The World of Animals

BEARS

Editor: Winwood Reade

From all my experience the conviction is pressed upon my mind that the grizzly-bear possesses a nature which, if taken in time and carefully improved, may be made the perfection of animal goodness.

JOHN CAPEN ADAMS

The World of Animals

BEARS

RICHARD PERRY

Published simultaneously by

Arco Publishing Company, Inc.
219 PARK AVENUE SOUTH, NEW YORK, N.Y. 10003

and

Arthur Barker Limited
5 WINSLEY STREET LONDON WI

Acknowledgements for Illustrations

The author and publishers are indebted to the following for permission to reproduce photographs in this book: Mr R. Allin and Bruce Coleman Ltd for the photograph on page 61; Mr T. Angermayer and Bruce Coleman Ltd for the photograph on page 90; Mr D. Bartlett, Armand Denis Productions and Bruce Coleman Ltd for the photograph on page 28; Mr F. W. Champion for the photographs on pages 25, 62; Mr S. Gillsater and Bruce Coleman Ltd for the photographs on pages 6, 19, 22, 27, 48, 50, 66, 72, 77, 86; Mr R. Kinne and Bruce Coleman Ltd for the photographs on pages 21, 24, 26, 42, 44 and 45, 67, 78; Mr C. J. Ott and Bruce Coleman Ltd for the photographs on pages 11, 17, 56, 80, 95; Mr W. L. Puchalski and Bruce Coleman Ltd for the photographs on pages 13, 15, 29, 57; Mr D. Robinson and Bruce Coleman Ltd for the photograph on page 55; Mr L. L. Rue and Bruce Coleman Ltd for the photographs on pages 18, 32 and 33, 34, 35, 36, 39, 53, 59, 69, 74, 82, 83, 84; Mr H. Sielmann for the photographs on pages 49, 63; Mr J. Simon and Bruce Coleman Ltd for the photographs on pages 14, 23, 54, 65; Mr W. Suschitzky for the photographs on pages 7, 9, 10, 31, 40, 58, 70, 89, 91, 92; Mr P. Wayre for the photographs on pages 8, 12, 16, 38; and Mr J. Van Wormer and Bruce Coleman Ltd for the photographs on pages 20, 51, 60, 64, 68. To the following publishers and authors for permission to quote from their books – George Allen & Unwin, *No Room for Bears* (1966) by F. Dufresne and Oxford University Press, *The Temple Tiger* (1952) by J. Corbett.

Library of Congress Catalog Number 73-77894
Standard Book Number 668-01845-3
Printed in Great Britain
Bound in Holland

Contents

A family of Alaskan bears watching for salmon

CHAPTER ONE

Their habitat

There are polar bears in the Arctic; black bears and brown bears (including the grizzlies) in North America; spectacled bears distributed sparsely through the Andes from the Caribbean to southern Peru; brown bears from western Europe to Kamchatka and from the Near East to Japan; black bears in the Himalayas and south-east Asia; sloth bears in India and Ceylon; and sun bears in Burma, Malaya and Sumatra.

The majority, polar bears excepted, are forest bears in greater or lesser degree, because although omnivorous in the broadest sense of the term, they are predominantly vegetarian, with enormous quantities of berries, fruits, nuts and grass forming an essential part of their diet.

Forests also provide secluded shelter in which he-bears can den-up in the winter and she-bears rear their cubs. This factor may govern their choice of habitat, as in the case of black bears in Manchuria concentrating in the deciduous forests where there is an abundance of large hollow poplars suitable for denning.

During the past two hundred years forests have also served as a refuge from man's incessant persecution; and one of the reasons for the large population of brown bears in Kamchatka is the dense cover of dwarf pine, alder and shrub that clothes much of the hills and is impassable to man during the summer months.

Their dependence on forests has not, however, prohibited bears from adapting themselves to a variety of habitats. American black bears are to be found from the tree limit in

European brown bear cubs

The full magnificence of a Kodiak bear

OPPOSITE: Sun bears are mainly arboreal

Some of the monstrous brown bears of Kodiak
Island stand over eleven feet erect

OPPOSITE: In search of roots, grizzlies shovel
the gravel aside like bulldozers

northern Canada and the glaciers and salmon streams of
Alaska and British Columbia to the cane-brakes of Louisiana's
lukewarm swamps and the searing heat of Mexico's northern
plateau. Brown bears are as at home in the latter habitat as
they are on the frozen tundras of Canada and Siberia, and
range from the forest floor to the snow line in the loftiest
mountain ranges of both Old and New Worlds.

A very few races of bears have made their permanent homes
outside the forests. Some of the so-called Himalayan black
bears inhabit Baluchistan's arid plateaus of rock and scrub,
and still more remarkably a southern race of the small black
or brownish spectacled bear (whose curious yellow or white
facial markings vary incongruously from one individual to
another, irrespective of age or sex) live in the excessively
parched mountainous region of northern Peru. There, rain
falls only rarely; animal life is restricted; and the sparse
vegetation consists mainly of cacti and small thornbushes,
with a few scattered thickets of trees in canyons and on higher
slopes. But in this near-desert spectacled bears are abroad
under the midday tropic sun, feeding on the *chapote*: that
pear-shaped fruit with a hard outer shell enclosing numerous
seeds; and are credibly reported to have been lassoed from
horseback at one time. Yet less than four hundred miles to the
north, another community of spectacled bears are inhabitants
of the montane rain forest, from which they venture out only
occasionally, either to climb above ten thousand feet to the
grasslands of the temperate zone, or to go down to the tropical
savannas and scrublands of the Andean foothills.

All bears can climb – even polar bears, if the almost sheer
side of an iceberg be substituted for the trunk of a tree; and the
large Himalayan black bears, which may grow to more than
six and a half feet and weigh four hundred pounds, obtain
much of their food in the tree-tops, as do the rather smaller
sloth bears. Nevertheless, there is a clear physical distinction
between the regular climbers – the black bears, sloth, spectacled and sun bears – and brown bears and polar bears: for
whereas the latter have hairy soles to their feet, those of climbing bears are naked, with a rough skin that enables them to
grip the bark of a tree, as do their sharp claws and the pro-
nounced inward curve of their paws. The curved claws, three
inches in length, of a sun bear, climbing with arms spread wide
across the trunk, hook into the slightest crevice; and he can

A sun bear stands only four or, at most, five
feet

indeed hang upside-down by his claws. To the Malays, this
smallest and most arboreal of the bears, standing only four or
at most five feet erect, and coal-black or brownish except for
silvery muzzle and ear-tips and the cream or orange 'rising-sun'
blazoned on his chest, is *basindo nan tenggil*: he who likes to
sit high. This is a reference perhaps to his habit, if caught out
in a heavy shower, of scuttling up the nearest tree and climbing out along a limb to a fork. There he pulls in leaves and
twigs beneath him, to form a mat on which he can lie with
his chin in the fork of the limb, his body along the length of
it, and all four legs hanging down.

A sloth bear can climb the smoothest bole, and a black
bear shin up a tall tree like a squirrel, corkscrewing round the
trunk in a series of leaps until reaching a branch.

Bears of the same species vary greatly in size from one
individual to another, and a large male American black bear
may be bulkier than a small female grizzly. But by and large,
brown bears are larger and heavier than black bears, averaging from five to eight feet in length and from three hundred
and fifty to a thousand pounds in weight; while the great
brown bears of western Alaska and its peninsulas, and of
Kodiak Island and the Kenai Peninsula reach a length of ten
feet, stand fifty-four inches at the shoulder, and weigh up to
sixteen hundred and fifty pounds. However, there is reasonable evidence that some polar bears grow to a length of
eleven feet and weigh two thousand pounds.

Thus the weight of brown bears, once they have grown to
maturity, is likely to prohibit them from climbing trees for
food, though even a grizzly can climb trees with low branches,
as a ranger in the Yellowstone National Park was surprised
to see one morning when a she-bear and two cubs were
clambering about an apple-tree. shaking off the apples.

Despite their inability to climb freely for food, most brown
bears are forest dwellers, and the largest population of them
inhabits the vast coniferous taiga of the USSR, especially
where the forest is interspersed with marsh and newly growing
burnt areas; though the more open country of the birchwood
steppes, that they still inhabit from White Russia to the Urals,
suits them better. In western Europe, where the few remaining
bears have been driven into remote mountainous areas, they
prefer mixed woods of conifers and especially beech or birch,
associated with a rich vegetation in the ravines or on the alpine

meadows above. Such habitats supply them not only with beechmast and hazel-nuts, berries, voles, ants and insects – in search of which they roll up the turves like a carpet – but also with great quantities of grass.

There is probably no necessity for tropical bears ever to venture out of their forests and jungles, in which food is available throughout the twelve months; and there is no evidence that either sun bears or sloth bears ever do so, though the former inhabit jungle at an altitude of five thousand feet in Borneo, and the latter the wooded foothills of the Himalayas. However, some USSR brown bears migrate seasonally in quest of berries to a height of eight or nine thousand feet: just as, in the Himalayas, he-bears of both brown and black species may climb in the early summer to the upper limits of the forest, some five thousand feet above their wintering valleys; there they pass out on to the bare hills and graze like cattle on the new grass, as the melting snows recede, or plough up great tracts of hillside in their search for roots and tubers. So too, the 'blue' bear of Tibet and Mongolia, though wintering in the mountainous beechwoods and bamboo jungles of Szechwan, passes the summer on the treeless steppes, grubbing up roots and tubers, digging voles and pikas (mouse-hares) out of their burrows, and hooking fish out of the streams.

European brown bears are forest dwellers

An American grizzly may be light brown or grizzled, almost golden, black or almost white, but characteristically silver-tipped; and there is a great difference in the field between the relatively small grizzly of what may be termed the USA hinterland east of the Rockies; and the mighty hump-shouldered 'silver-tip' of Alaska, we are concerned only with three obvious races of grizzlies –

First, those mighty brown bears of Alaska's west coast, where the mountains tower steeply from the shores of the Pacific, though receding at the heads of the numerous bays to form large flats and meadows. These 'meadows' are the bears' main grazing grounds with the sanctuary of the forest always close at hand.

Second, the barren-ground grizzlies of the Yukon and the Northwest Territories which roam the tundras and steep hills that are almost devoid of vegetation, save for wind-dwarfed alders and low clumps of sedge, though the broad gravel-bars

European brown bears prefer mixed woods of conifers and beech or birch

OPPOSITE: American black bears display an extraordinary range of colouring

15

A sun bear excavating for grubs

OPPOSITE: Typical grizzly country on barren-grounds

The mighty hump-shouldered 'silver-tip' with six-inch claws

that break up the rivers into mazes carry a dense growth of pea-vine, and the bears shovel the gravel aside like bulldozers in search of the tuberous roots.

And third, the grizzlies of the USA hinterland's rolling uplands, where open prairies are interspersed with rocky ridges and densely-wooded thickets. The latter hold abundant supplies of food, together with sunning places and shady retreats in which the bears can lie-up, free from the plague of flies and mosquitoes. They never stay long above the timber line, and if food is plentiful they may range no further than six or nine miles from their base, though in the days when they followed the buffalo herds, their range might perhaps have been extended to as much as sixty miles. But, like most animals, bears do not normally wander outside their habitual range – witness those grizzlies in British Columbia which, after being transported to points up to thirty-eight miles from the Glacier National Park, duly found their way back to the park and resumed the customary round.

Finally, there is the one bear whose habitat includes no forest – the polar bear. But he, too, may be a close relative of the European brown bear. The polar bear is the one bear whom it would be superfluous to describe, since there has never been a record of one that was not white or creamy-white. This mono-colouring of the polar bear is in striking contrast to the extraordinary range of colouring exhibited by brown and especially black bears. An American black bear may have three differently coloured cubs in one litter. Brown bears may be brown, ash-brown, rust-coloured, cream or even black, while the pale blond fur of the Tibetan blue bear may include black hairs frosted with silver or slate-grey tips, producing the illusion of blue fur. Black bears may be glossy black (with a white blotch on the chest if American, or a prominent white horseshoe if Asian), any shade of brown, yellowish, silvery or cinnamon, while some individuals of the small glacier or blue bear of Alaska may be maltese-blue, with blue and black cubs in the same litter. Kermode's bear in its diversified habitat of forest, rock and glacier in British Columbia, may be black, chestnut-red, orange, yellow with dark stripes, or pure white except for slight buffing on head and saddle.

There cannot be any stretch of shore on the periphery of the North Polar basin that, through the centuries, has not been trodden by polar bears; nor any substantial ice-fields they have not traversed to the very Pole itself, for a she-bear and cub have been encountered as far north as 88°. If most other bears are dependent for their living on the fruits of the forest, polar bears are dependent for theirs on the ice-fields – for Arctic waters swarm with those planktonic crustaceans which the whalermen knew as *krill*. The polar cod feed on the krill. Seals feed on the cod, and bears on seals.

Polar bears are perennial wanderers with the pack-ice that is for ever drifting with winds and currents clockwise round the Pole. Sailing on bergs, rafting on floes, they are carried from one ice-field to another and from Arctic island to mainland shore, on leisurely voyages that certainly exceed a thousand miles range. Some bears pass out of Arctic waters and into the North Atlantic or through Bering Strait into the Bering Sea. When the pack extends abnormally far south, as it did in the springs of 1965 and 1966, then a few polar bears are carried to such southerly outposts as Iceland or the northern islands of Japan. Such wanderers are almost certainly doomed, for when the pack melts and breaks up in the summer they are left stranded on their islands. Although powerful and indefatigable swimmers, and prepared to swim fifteen or twenty miles out to an iceberg – a favourite resort of seals – polar bears in general dislike sea voyages, and will detour long distances overland rather than swim across quite narrow stretches of water from one ice-field to another.

There cannot be any stretch of shore on the North Polar basin that has not been trodden by polar bears

19

CHAPTER TWO

As vegetarians

Hard put to know how to put in his time

Consider the sloth bear who lives in a favourable habitat of dense jungle. His headquarters is a clump of bamboo or some rocky retreat of tumbled boulders, preferably with a cave where the temperature remains constant, and in which he can shelter from heavy rains, intense heat and flies. From dawn until shortly before sunset he passes the hours buzzing and humming while sucking his paws. Why do bears, and especially sloth bears and sun bears, suck their paws? – possibly because much of their food is sticky or juicy or fishy, or because there is a sticky secretion between their pads. Possibly it is a psychological habit. That marvellous observer of bears, William H. Wright, hunter and prospector in the mid-western Rockies for thirty years at the turn of the century, noted that in contrast to the industrious grizzly, who is forever searching and digging laboriously for food and methodically burying it for future use, the playboy black bear – the Happy Hooligan – who never caches food, always appears to be hard put to know how to fill in his time:

I have seen one rip a piece off an old stump, sniff for bugs, find none, stand undecided for a few minutes, and then walk up to a tree and draw itself upright against the trunk, stretching like a cat. It then sat down at the foot of the tree and scratched its ear. It then got up and started off aimlessly, but, happening to straddle a low bush in its path and liking the feeling of the branches against its belly, it walked backward and forward half a dozen times to repeat the sensation. Then it started back the way it had come and smelling a mouse under a log, suddenly woke up. It tried to move the log and failed. It dug a bit at one end but gave that up. It then tried again, very hard this time, to turn the log over, and the log giving way suddenly, the bear turned a complete somersault backward, but instantly recovered itself and rushed around with the most ludicrous haste to see if the mouse had gotten away. It hadn't. After he had eaten the mouse he didn't know what to do next. There was a fallen tree nearby and he got up on the trunk and walked the length of it. Then he turned round and walked back again to the butt. Here he stood and looked straight ahead of him. Then he climbed down backward very slowly and carefully as if he were afraid of falling (the log was perhaps eighteen inches high), and walked round to examine a place where the upturned roots had left a hole in the earth. Finally he sat down and began 'weaving'. That is to say, he began swinging his head from side to side, as one often sees a bear do behind the bars of a zoo. There is nothing more expressive of hopeless ennui.

During cool weather the sloth bear usually sleeps outside in tall grass or under a tree; and being well insulated by a thick, shaggy coat of coarse hair falling like a mane over neck and shoulders, he is more tolerant of the sun than some jungle animals, such as the tiger, and may even fall asleep in it. But, like the latter, he is a thirsty beast and must have a constant water-supply available. His first act on coming abroad in the evening is to drink, and if his regular source of water fails, he digs for it in the dried-up bed of a stream or travels many miles to another water hole. In cool cloudy weather he may stir abroad at any hour of the day when his favourite fruits are in season; and in places remote from human disturbance he is, like so many wild animals, less nocturnal in his habits, nocturnalism being a defence against man's persecution.

Fruit and insects comprise the bulk of his food. In the cool season *ber* trees are in berry, and later, when the *mowha* is in bloom, the ground beneath a grove of these trees is carpeted with their fleshy, heavily-scented flowers. By day the villagers collect the fallen petals, from which they distil the bulk of their spirits. By night the bears are no less avid for them, and one hour of moonlight may bring a succession of seven bears rushing from tree to tree and then shuffling off to another grove – not a minute to be lost! In the hot season fig trees, *bel* and ebony trees are all fruiting, and night after night the bears visit the fig trees in regular succession, either shaking the fruit down or climbing for it. After the heavy rains of the

OVERLEAF (LEFT): Giant Alaskan brown bears salmon fishing at the waterfalls at McNeil river, Alaska

OVERLEAF (RIGHT): A grizzly may not break out of his den until April or May

The sloth bear is well insulated by a thick shaggy coat of coarse hair

A sun bear's long tongue serves to lap up ants and termites

monsoon, those sloth bears near villages raid the ripening crops of sugar-cane and maize, and if the villagers are tapping a stand of date-palms, climb these in order to drink the toddy from the catching-pots. It is not so much the loss of their toddy that troubles the villagers as the number of pots the bears break.

During the monsoon, insects and larvae are abundant under stones and fallen logs, and in the bark and crevices of trees. All bears have a highly developed sense of smell, and a sloth bear can locate a grub three feet below ground, and dig down with remarkable rapidity to the tunnels of the large white larvae of dung-beetles and longicorns. But most sought after are termites, which are also taken by black bears and sun bears. With his immensely powerful ivory-white claws, four inches in length, the sloth bear breaks down or burrows into a termite mound until he reaches its core. Then, with prodigious huffs and puffs, he blows away the finer dust and sucks the ants out of their galleries. A sloth bear's powers of suction are further increased by the absence of the middle pair of incisors in his upper jaw permitting the passage of air through the gap.

The hot season in India is also the season of honey. Thus, in addition to harvesting figs, the sloth bear is then on the lookout for the combs of the small forest-bee in hollow trees, and also for the huge combs of the large rock-bee, which hang in clusters from the branches of trees or from the undersides of rocks. The latter he knocks down to the ground – possibly deliberately, for in the darkness the bees tend to buzz around the site of the comb rather than fly down in pursuit of the raiding bear – but the combs of forest-bees cannot of course be knocked down. They must be taken the hard way, and a Himalayan black bear can be heard bawling with the pain of the stings implanted in his muzzle, but nonetheless persisting in his 'honey-combing'.

If a bear meets with problems in his search for food, he solves them intelligently and with ingenuity. V. K. Arseniev, who explored the Manchurian taiga in the early years of this century, watched a black bear attempting to get a hive of bees in a tall lime tree that was growing almost flush against a rock:

He was standing on his hind legs. The stones prevented him thrusting his paw into the hole in the tree. He was not a patient bear, and was shaking the tree with all his might and growling with irritation. A cloud of bees was humming round him, stinging him on the head. He kept rubbing his head with his paws, uttering a high-pitched little scream, rolling on the ground, and going back once more to his work. His antics were most comical. At last he was tired. He squatted on the ground in an almost human manner, opened his mouth, and stared at the tree, evidently thinking it out. He sat like that for a couple of minutes. Then he suddenly sat up, ran to the tree, and climbed it to the top. Then he squeezed himself in between the tree and the rock and, pressing with all four paws against the rock, began to push with his back against the tree with all his might. The tree yielded a little. But evidently it rather hurt his back. Then he altered his position and, putting his back against the rock, began to push the tree with all his might. Presently the tree gave a rending sound, split, and crashed to the ground.

That was just what the bear wanted. All he had to do now was to clean open the nest and collect the honey.

Bears are traditionally gluttons for honey. Black bears in the mountains of California are so persistent in their raids on domestic beehives that these are often placed on high platforms or surrounded with electrified barriers; and perhaps those brown bears who recently astonished villagers in the Sar

With his immensely powerful claws a sloth bear burrows into termite mounds

Planina mountains of Yugoslavia by climbing telegraph poles may have been deluded by the humming of the wires into supposing that bees were nesting on the poles.

Berries, fruits and nuts, especially acorns and beechmast; the buds and leaves of maples, aspens and rowans; roots such as the Indian turnip, that intolerably pungent arum; wild white clover and the bulbs of the dog-foot violet; ripening maize; ants, termites and the larvae of beetles, crickets and grasshoppers; frogs and toads; birds and their eggs; mice, chipmunks, ground-squirrels and marmots, an occasional porcupine, trout and salmon – these, according to season, make up the varied diet of an American black bear. Ants he laps up by the thousand as they swarm out of their broken tunnels or, if they are vinegar ants, plunges one paw deep into a 'hill', stirs it round, withdraws it, and then stretches out with his front paws extended to the base of the hill, and waits for the frenzied ants to swarm over them and be licked up. He is as indifferent to their acetate as he is to the stings of bees, wasps and hornets. The porcupine he turns over with a quick flip of his paw, tears open the unprotected underpart, and scoops the animal out of its skin; though a clumsy or careless bear may receive a faceful of quills and, with lips bristling with them and mouth too swollen with festering sores to eat, he must inevitably starve to death. He robs the squirrels of their hoards of nuts, as the black bear of Manchuria robs the chipmunks of theirs. If frost does not loosen the nuts early enough he climbs the trees and either shakes them down or tears off a branch and eats the nuts on the ground.

So long as food supplies are plentiful the individual black bear ranges around his particular forest within a radius of fifteen miles or so of his base, bathing at frequent intervals in hot weather when flies are troublesome or when shedding his hair – just as the grizzlies in the Yellowstone National Park bathe in the hot sulphur springs – and rarely remaining long in a waterless region. But there are of course innumerable regional variations in habits and diet. Himalayan black bears come abroad at dusk from hollow trees or dry caves to raid orchards for apples and pears, apricots, peaches, mulberries and walnuts; while those that winter in the rhododendron groves and beech forests of the Tibetan-Chinese borderlands venture out in the summer to raid the ripening corn in the fields that are cultivated to a height of several thousand feet up

Berries are an essential seasonal item in a black bear's diet

the steep hillsides towering above the narrow valleys of Szechwan.

Berries are an essential item in the diet of all bears. In August, ninety per cent of a Yukon grizzly's food may consist of berries, especially those of the thornless soap-berry, so called by the Indians because of the bright red froth produced when the berries are crushed. When feasting on berries, they either straddle the bushes and small trees, forcing them over, or hook the branches down with their paws, half breaking them.

The considerable wastage of berries falling from the bears' half-open mouths attracts numbers of ground-squirrels, chipmunks and mice. Grubbing for small rodents, whether mice or voles, pikas or ground-squirrels, must take up a considerable part of a brown bear's time; and hardly more profitable, one would think, are the hours he devotes to hunting ground-squirrels, whose burrows and runways are usually among rocks or under the roots of large trees, or in similarly inconvenient retreats for bears. His great strength and immense claws, five or six inches in length, enable a grizzly to

In July many polar bears, drifting with the pack-ice, land on islands

dig deeper and faster than the short-clawed black bear, and the quantity of soil he excavates when hunting for ground-squirrels is hardly credible. Vast stretches of grassy slopes in Alaska may be pitted with holes, some large enough to hold a piano, from which hibernating ground-squirrels have been rooted out. But many burrows are not occupied. Dr Pearson, watching one grizzly digging furiously for fifteen minutes without success, excavating with alternate scoops of his fore-claws, concluded that hunting ground-squirrels must be a most frustrating activity for a bear. However, although he never once saw a bear pull a squirrel out of its burrow, he did observe that when the bear removed his paw a squirrel might rush out and be pounced on. All bears can strike with lightning rapidity and precision, using their claws like fingers and manipulating delicately with them. That the relatively small sun bear should be able to pick up a single grain of rice with a claw three inches long is not perhaps so wonderful: but a grizzly, powerful enough to heave over large boulders, huffing and puffing as he flings aside the rocks sheltering a twenty-pound marmot, can also pick up small objects precisely with two claws, or even with one; and he is regularly to be seen turning over stones for such minute game as beetles, ants and crickets.

In July when polar bears, drifting with the pack, land on islands and Arctic shores, they become vegetarian. Such a change of diet is no doubt beneficial, after months of seal blubber and carrion, and typically ursine in its composition of grass, sedge and sorrel, lichens and mosses, mushrooms and, above all, immense quantities of crowberries, cranberries and blueberries. One bear may indeed feed solely on berries for weeks, until his muzzle and hindquarters are stained blue with their juice. No less typically ursine is the quest for rodents – in this case those courageous little beasts, lemmings, which a she-bear will dig up and toss to her cubs. During these summer weeks ashore polar bears are as omnivorous as other bears, scavenging for dead seabirds at the base of nesting cliffs and digging puffins out of their burrows, robbing the nests of ducks and geese (as Kamchatka bears also do), filching foxes and ptarmigan from traps, or clawing up shellfish along the beaches.

A sun bear can pick up a single grain of rice with one claw

CHAPTER THREE

As predators

Although most bears are primarily vegetarians their habitats are plentifully supplied with plants and fruits for only five or six months out of the twelve. In order to survive they must therefore also be predators and scavengers. Indeed there is not much doubt that all bears would prefer a predominantly high-meat diet. A sloth bear will gnaw cattle-bones or devour the carcase of a muntjac deer. The relatively small spectacled bears are mainly vegetarian on such foods as green maize cobs and the fruits of omero, guavae and various kinds of palms, for which they will climb eighty or a hundred feet and bring down the fruit stalk, or break down the young trees in order to tear open the green stalk and eat the unopened leaves in the interior. Yet they too are reported to kill the young of llamas, deer and cattle. But forest bears, despite their immense strength, are not physically equipped to prey on large mammals; and since they are unable to secure sufficient food in the form of rodents and carrion, they are obliged to be omnivorous. Only the polar bear has solved the problem of being a carnivore by learning to prey on seals. It is a problem that has defeated other bears over a period of thousands of years.

The flattened, blunt-edged and well-developed cheek-teeth of black bears are clearly adapted to the mastication of hard, fibrous vegetable substances such as roots, grass and nuts. Nevertheless American black bears not only prey extensively on rodents but also kill young deer and antelope and even moose calves, when they can catch them. When beaver were

The European brown bear is predominantly a vegetarian

numerous, a black bear would stalk stealthily from one lodge to the next, intent on ambushing any individual preoccupied with tree-cutting or dam-building activities.

A vegetarian may be compelled to become a predator either by hunger or by being driven into close association with relatively defenceless domestic stock, when its natural sources of food are curtailed by man's encroachment on its habitat. In such circumstances American black bears may kill lambs and calves and especially piglets; and in the days when the plains of the West were littered with the carcases of sheep and cattle, they were considered useful scavengers until, inevitably, some individuals graduated from scavenging carrion to becoming regular sheep killers – like the she-bear with two cubs who took to killing a sheep every other evening. Himalayan black bears resident near villages kill sheep, goats and even fully grown cattle, and also prey upon such large deer as the Kashmir stag; while Jim Corbett (of man-eating tiger fame) witnessed a black bear carrying off a tiger's kill in the latter's absence.

During the hungry season of spring, when European brown bears have used up the reserves of fat upon which they drew during their winter hibernation, and are reduced to scavenging for anything edible, whether it be frozen berries preserved under the snow, or ants, or carrion in the form of reindeer carcases, a few individuals may attack the young of wild boar, roe or elk, and even adult elk and reindeer. The deer they stalk noiselessly, to the manner born, as if to emphasize that a bear is truly a carnivore and only a vegetarian on sufferance. Occasionally domestic cattle are attacked, and in those parts of the Russian taiga where the village stock pasture in the forest, brown bears may become considerable killers of cattle and horses. In like manner approximately one in twenty of those brown bears wandering in the summer high above the tree-line in Bulgaria become habitual sheep killers on the alpine pastures – though the kill amounts only to about one sheep per bear per year. So too, Himalayan brown bears may prey on sheep, goats and ponies when the latter are driven up to the mountain pastures in the summer, but such predation is not general. In some instances, no doubt, it is 'accidental', as in the case of that Italian she-bear and cub who, as recently as 1965, fell through a mountain lean-to in the Abruzzi National Park and killed, in their panic, every one of seventy folded sheep. Certainly, when brown bears were common in Europe they were often to be seen 'grazing' harmlessly with cattle, sheep and goats in alpine meadows, or with chamois, or among herds of reindeer on the Scandinavian fjelds. Some of the still considerable population of bears in the Caucasus are based in sheep-farming areas, but they neither prey on the sheep nor trouble the shepherds. One may indeed be resting in a cave, with sheep grazing outside.

Naturally, such large bears as grizzlies are more habitually predacious, though it has been estimated that eighty or ninety per cent of a barren-ground grizzly's food is vegetable. A grizzly can gallop with rolling gait as fast as a good horse over a stretch of from fifty to a hundred yards, faster over rough country, and has in fact been timed to do 30 mph. Although the Indians' starving outwintering ponies were easy prey for him, he could not run down the deer and buffalo, whose earth-shaking herds he followed in order to scavenge on the carcases of dead beasts. But he could catch the old and sick by stalking them on his belly until close enough for a final furious rush in fifteen-foot bounds. In this way he still kills an occasional adult caribou or reindeer in a stampeding herd. Nevertheless it is the young caribou, and also wild sheep, that are his main prey, though by the time the calves are two or three weeks old they are too agile to be caught. Grizzlies and caribou, however, can sometimes be seen grazing in close proximity, without the latter displaying undue anxiety. Barren-ground grizzlies, and also polar bears, are known to kill an occasional musk-ox, despite the almost impregnable 'defence-in-square' formed by the bulls (packed so closely that they almost tread on each other's hooves), and grouped around the cows and younger beasts, with the calves sheltering beneath their mothers' shaggy bellies. With heads lowered the protective screen of bulls presents a solid wall of horn against any predator.

Even the gigantic moose occasionally falls a victim to a grizzly. One has been seen dragging the carcase of a bull moose, weighing upwards of a ton. In his *Mammals of North America* Victor H. Cahalane describes how one summer day a fisherman in Yellowstone Park was astonished to see a bull moose dash out of the forest with a grey grizzly clinging and tearing at its hip. The moose succeeded, however, in shaking off its attacker at the edge of the stream and escaped into

Tender, sometimes severe when need be: European brown bear

deep water, leaving the frustrated bear to rage up and down the bank for some hours.

The coming of the white man's flocks and herds provided grizzlies with a permanent source of easy meat, and as the herds of deer and buffalo were decimated, so a luxury often became a necessity. When preying on cattle a grizzly would adopt the ruse of rolling and tumbling about in the grass, while the herd stood around, bawling crazily. Then, when a long-horned cow finally made a rush at this distracting object, he would seize her by the throat. Sheep were still easier meat, as an old-timer, John Muir, witnessed when he spent a night at a shepherd's camp:

The show made by the wall of fire when it was blazing in its prime was magnificent: the illumined trees round about relieved against solid darkness, and the two thousand sheep lying down in one grey mass, sprinkled with gloriously brilliant gems, the effect of the firelight in their eyes. It was nearly midnight when the pair of freebooters arrived. They walked boldly through a gap in the fire circle, killed two sheep, carried them out, and vanished in the dark woods, leaving ten dead in a pile, trampled down and smothered against the corral fence.

When brown bears become predators or carrion eaters they often, as we have seen, cache the carcases. And Arseniev relates a remarkable instance of how, within half an hour of shooting one of two Manchurian brown bears, its companion had covered its body with a heap of earth, stones and logs. A grizzly may hide the remains of a moose or wild sheep, feeding on the carcase at intervals and guarding it fiercely; or bury it with fresh earth, and return to it two or three days later. Theodore Roosevelt watched one grizzly preparing to bury the carcase of a moose, after dragging it a hundred yards, and described how he would twist the carcase around with the utmost ease, sometimes taking it in his fore-paws and half lifting, half shoving it.

In the harsh habitat of the Barguzinski Nature Reserve around Lake Baikal, where snow may lie throughout the summer, the brown bears range through dense mountain forest, birch and juniper, down to the lake-side's salt-pans and mossy bogs of cranberry underbrush and stunted larches. To their seasonal diet of juniper cones, berries, roots and caddisfly larvae these Baikal bears add spawning salmon; and during the summer months salmon is the staple food not only

Salmon is a staple food of Alaskan and Kamchatkan bears

of the large population of brown bears of Kamchatka, who will migrate great distances to other rivers if the salmon run fails in their own country, but also of the large brown bears in Alaska and the western Rockies, and occasionally of black bears in very shallow streams. Indeed the range of the Alaskan brown bears coincides closely with that of the spawning grounds of five different kinds of Pacific salmon, and may well have been responsible for the extraordinary density of approximately one bear to the square mile on the sixteen hundred square miles of Admiralty Island (Khutz-n'hu: Bears' Fort) off south-east Alaska – an island of dense forests of spruce and hemlock, whose windfalls lie across one another to a depth of five or ten feet.

It is interesting to note that every year, according to William Wright, the grizzlies of Idaho descend from the hills and high ridges to the streams a couple of weeks *before* the salmon are due to run up from the sea. Their method of fishing is to sit on the bank of a stream and watch the riffles up which the salmon struggle to force a passage, and then when one is halfway up, dash into the water and with a sweep of a paw hurl the fish ten or twenty feet beyond the bank. The bear then hurries ashore to eat it, or kill it, and returns to the stream to catch another. In less than an hour one grizzly might scoop out as many as seventeen fish, and then, instead of eating them, pile them together and bury them.

But this is not the technique employed by Alaskan bears. Allen Hasselborg, who lived and hunted on Admiralty Island for some thirty years, never saw salmon flipped out in this manner. No, your Alaskan bear wades out to a gravel bar and fishes in the shallows where the water is not more than a couple of feet deep, plunging and crashing about amid cascades of spray, endeavouring to pin down a wildly darting salmon with his paw, or seize it with a lightning strike of open jaws. A Kamchatkan bear may stand in the water and wait for a salmon to swim past, or squat down with only his head above water, or swim out into a lake and dive down through the crystal-clear water above a spring, to which the salmon are attracted, and seize one under water.

Nor does the bear neglect other fishermen's spoils, dragging a net with its catch of salmon up into the woods, or trailing off with an angler's string of trout. He also fishes by night.

No doubt his fishing technique is only acquired by much practice. Among Frank Dufresne's many experiences during most of forty years in Alaska, recounted in *No Room for Bears* – was one of watching two cubs trying to catch salmon, wading in up to their necks in the lower reaches below a rapids, where it would be easiest for them to grasp their catch. When their attempts met with no success their mother strode into the water, immersed her head, and came up with a fish dangling from her jaws. Followed by the squealing cubs, she carried it to a gravel bar, laid a paw on its head and with one slash of her teeth ripped the skin off one side. After the bickering cubs had stripped the pink flesh off that side she yanked the skin off the other side and ate with the cubs.

Some bears tire of an exclusive diet of salmon before the latter have finished spawning, and begin to browse the blueberries growing near the beaches. When these have been stripped, they gradually work their way up into the mountains, through successively ripening crops of berries, the latest of which they harvest before denning up for the winter. In like manner, the Kamchatka bears may leave the rivers in August, in order to feast on red-currants and crowberries, and subsequently on rowan berries and the seeds of the dwarf pine cones.

Other Alaskan bears, however, remain by the pools until the salmon have finished spawning, and clean up the now decomposing bodies of dead fish.

Polar bears rarely eat fish, though on those infrequent occasions when one happens to find itself beside a salmon stream, a few spawning fish may be taken. Polar bears, more than other bears perhaps, are the prisoners of their environment, the pack-ice. Fortunately, however, pack-ice is also the habitat of several kinds of seals. The almost total absence of polar bears off the northern coasts of the Canadian Arctic islands, or off the mainland of eastern Siberia, is due to the phenomenon that the inshore ice on those coasts does not break up every summer and provide the leads of open water that are essential to seals. Where the pack is in constant motion, often breaking up even during the winter freeze-up, as it does off Alaska and north-west Greenland or Spitzbergen or Franz Josef Land, the resulting leads are attractive to seals and therefore bears.

All bears are good swimmers and may take to the water

The bear would then hurry ashore to eat it

OPPOSITE (ABOVE): Does a high-protein diet of salmon account for the great size of Alaskan brown bears?

OPPOSITE: A grizzly may cache a number of fish instead of eating them

when wounded. There are records of an American black bear swimming five miles and of a Kamchatkan she-bear and two cubs swimming for several miles across a lake. Alaskan bears are much in the water, and on a gale-swept day when the turbid grey waters of the Bering Sea were smashing in great frothing combers to hiss across the sands of a beach on Unimak Island, Dufresne watched two yearling bears romping on the Pacific's edge, dashing in and out, snatching bits of kelp and flotsam and tossing them to one another:

Time after time they dodged from under with not a second to spare before a curling wave thundered down on the spot where they'd been. They came a cropper finally when they seized and tugged at a bulky object and were buried under an enormous foaming breaker. Then they emerged like drowned rats, fought the undertow, and dragged what appeared to be the bloated carcass of a sea lion high and dry.

If polar bears and brown bears are indeed related, then it was perhaps not too great a change from romping in the sea and fishing salmon streams to seal hunting among the ice-fields;

35

and for much of the year seals are the polar bear's main source of food. In the autumn, however, a herd of white whales or narwhals, fishing inshore, may find themselves cut off from the sea by a sudden freeze-up and confined to an ever-shrinking stretch of water, known to the Eskimos as a *saugssat*. As the ice encroaches on the lead, so the whales become desperate for breathing space, and a bear may take advantage of their plight to leap in and kill one or more of them. Such is his enormous strength that though these small whales may be fifteen feet in length and weigh eight hundred pounds, he is still able to drag his kill out on to the ice.

During the almost permanent darkness of the Arctic winter from November to January those polar bears that have not denned up have considerable difficulty in locating seals. Should they find themselves in a poor sealing area, then they must support life by scavenging. Carrion is their main standby – the carcases of seals and walruses or of a whale, even of another bear. One he-bear may pass an entire winter eating out the cadaver of a walrus or whale, kept company by glaucous gulls, ravens and those jackals of the Arctic, the beautiful smoke-blue or silver polar foxes, little larger than house-cats. Almost every sealing or scavenging bear is accompanied by one or more foxes, intent on feasting on the left-overs from his kills or, at worst, on undigested matter in his droppings. In this association between fox and bear – which is not entirely free from danger to the fox, who may venture too close to a carcase while the bear is eating and be killed by a swipe from his paw – the bear does all the work; for while he is conducting his lengthy stalk, the fox curls up to sleep on a convenient berg or hummock.

Although all kinds of seals are hunted by polar bears their chief prey are the relatively small ringed seals, which seldom weigh more than two hundred pounds. Throughout the summer those bears who have elected to stay out on the ice, or have not drifted ashore with the pack, hunt seals in the open leads, especially the young ones sun-basking on the floes. But seals are no easy prey. Only the young and inexperienced will sun-bathe near any hummock that could afford cover to a bear; while all the adults lie with their heads away from the wind and their eyes to leeward, and none will nap for more than a couple of minutes at a stretch. Climbing a hummock on the ice, or rearing up on his hind-legs, a sealing bear initially locates his prey by sight. Thereafter he takes infinite precautions, and the seal may be only a black spot on the white ice when he sets off on his stalk with immense care and stealth, throwing himself full-length when still some hundreds of yards distant and pulling himself along by his front paws a few yards at a time, or pushing with his hind paws, with his forelegs doubled under his chest. The instant the seal raises its head after a brief nap, the bear 'freezes', and his humped yellowish hindquarters are barely distinguishable from other irregularities on the ice. Only his black nose and small dark eyes stand out, and both Eskimo and white hunters affirm that a stalking bear will cover his nose with one paw, or push a piece of ice along in front of it.

Foot by foot the bear creeps up to the seal. Then, when within twelve or fifteen feet, he launches himself at it, in one or more lightning bounds, and strikes it with his paw. After licking up the blood gushing from its wounds, he pulls the carcase three or four feet back from the edge of the ice, in order to avoid the possibility of it slipping back into the water, and settles down to his meal. From ten to forty pounds of blubber at a sitting usually satisfies a bear, and when young seals are to be had for the taking, he may merely crush one pup's head, take a few mouthfuls of skin and blubber from its back, and amble on to kill another.

When the ice thickens in the autumn to a depth of more than four inches, the seals are obliged to settle down in one locality in order to keep a number of breathing holes open permanently throughout the winter. At this time, the polar bears must exercise all their skill in locating these *aglos* and in catching the seals when they pop up to breathe at irregular intervals. Having located an *aglo* with his phenomenally sensitive nose, which enables him to wind carrion or burning blubber at distances of ten miles or more, a sealing bear scrapes away the snow and the upper layer of ice above the *aglo*, until the latter is large enough for him to insert his broad paw. Then he sits back and waits for the seal to surface, which it is likely to do every seven or eight minutes, though not necessarily at the hole that the bear is watching. If it does pop up at the right hole, then the bear pounces on its head with teeth and claws and hauls it out on to the ice.

Normally, the head and tail of the salmon are not eaten

37

CHAPTER FOUR

In winter dens

All pregnant she-bears in temperate and Arctic regions retire into dens for periods of several weeks or months during the winter. All bear cubs are remarkably small at birth, no larger than rats or guinea-pigs, and less than 1/200 or 1/350 the weight of their mothers. They are also hairless, blind for the first few weeks, and cannot balance on their hind legs until some six weeks old. It is evident therefore that polar bear cubs, to take an extreme case, could not survive the long polar winter, when temperatures fall as low as −50°F or −60°F, without some special shelter in a habitat devoid of all natural cover. This, then, is one reason why bears den-up. In the tropics a permanent retreat is not necessary, for the cubs require shelter only for a short time after birth. The sloth bear's cave or earth in a bank, the sun bear's hollow log or tree platform, afford their cubs protection against excessive heat or heavy rain.

There is another reason. The further north a bear lives the greater his difficulty in obtaining adequate food supplies during the winter: but he can avoid starvation by denning-up for variable periods, and subsist during these periods of retreat on his reserves of fat. Thus the actual date and duration of denning among he-bears, barren she-bears and she-bears with yearling cubs will vary from one individual to another and from one year to the next according to the availability of food supplies and the severity of the winter. Fat bears will be in their dens by the middle of October, others not until the middle of December. Some Kamchatkan and

Three months old black bear: a cub cannot balance on its hind legs until six weeks old

OPPOSITE: The long curved claws of a sun bear hook into the slightest crevices

39

All bear cubs are extraordinarily small at birth

Alaskan bears, for example, can find food, despite deep snow, as late as December by fishing near springs. And the period of denning may be broken. Even in the northern Rockies black bears may emerge temporarily during spells of warmer weather, and yearling brown bears in Manchuria may leave their dens from time to time independently of their mother, even after snow has fallen.

Some Himalayan black bears, by descending several thousand feet from their high summer feeding grounds to the valleys below, find food available throughout the winter, and are not obliged to den-up. Some grizzlies and black bears in the more southerly parts of their respective ranges also find it unnecessary to den-up, or do so only for a few days or for a week or two at a time during January and February; in a good beechmast year, brown bears in the Carpathians may not den-up at all. Tropical bears never have to do so. Nevertheless, the habit of going into dens may persist among some races of bears who live in regions where it is now physically unnecessary. The rather large black bears of Florida (and also the Mexican grizzly) are a case in point: despite the fact that the Florida winter is normally warm, and food in the form of their favourite palmetto berries abundant, they are still accustomed to den-up from early January until mid-March.

Low temperatures do not control the date of denning-up among forest bears, for by the early autumn they are fully equipped with a dense under-coat beneath the outer guard-hair. Heavy snow-falls, blanketing the vegetation, determine the date. Nevertheless, there is an awareness of a denning-up timetable for, come the middle of November, brown bears in Europe and Manchuria will den-up, even if heavy snow has still not fallen and although food supplies are still plentiful. But pregnant she-bears will always be the first to prospect for dens, and after them she-bears with yearling cubs.

Despite the harshness of their environment, some male and barren female polar bears may not den-up at all, or only for a week or two at a time during blizzards or periods of very low temperatures when they are unable to hunt seals or locate the carcases of whales or walruses. These bears may pass the entire winter hunting seals far out at the rough ice-edge of large areas of open water. It is a fair assumption that some of these 'out-winterers', whether polar or forest bears, are those that have been unable to put on enough fat during the summer and autumn, for they are almost always in poor condition, and a bear is not in a suitable state for 'hibernation' if it has not stored up sufficient reserves of fat on which to subsist during the period of retreat. It cannot be said that bears neglect any opportunity of feeding day and night, whenever hungry, during the summer. Nevertheless, the tempo of feeding speeds up in the autumn, as it does with true hibernators, controlled perhaps by what can be termed a thermostatic adjustment by the hypothalmus – that thickening of the nervous tissue connecting the cerebral hemispheres with the remainder of the brain. However that may be, most bears are very fat by the late autumn, with three or four inches of 'blubber' under their skins – fat enough to rest and fast for a week or two before retiring to their dens.

The actual sites of dens, and the dens themselves, are very variable. A den may be no more than that small hole in the snow or among the pressure-ice occupied for a few days during a blizzard by a male polar bear. The den of a European brown

A young sun bear

bear may amount only to a bed of moss and twigs, on which he curls up or lies on his side with nose buried in paws (the low-hanging branches of a dense spruce making an excellent shelter) and allows himself to be snowed over. A hole dug in a bank, a hollow stump, a large ant-hill – any of these will serve a brown bear for a den. As the retreat is covered with snow, so a cave is formed within by the heat given off from the bear's body; eventually this 'den' can only be located by the small frosted aperture above the sleeping bear's nose. In the rigorous conditions of Siberia, however, a more substantial den is required – a cave in the mountains, or a deep hole excavated by the bear himself on the southern slope of a hill where the snow melts soonest in the spring. Such a site contrasts with that preferred by grizzlies in the northern Rockies. The latter excavate holes ten or twelve feet deep between the wide-spreading roots of trees in heavy spruce and hemlock forest, or among the rocks on northern slopes where the deepest snow falls and where drifts accumulate. Then, after raking in quantities of leaves and dried grasses for bedding, the grizzlies seal up draught-holes with earth and stones. A Californian grizzly will excavate a den among the chaparral in a canyon, with an entrance passage, three to four feet in diameter and six to ten feet long, terminating in a round chamber thickly carpeted with leaves and grass.

The denning places of American black bears differ little from those of brown bears. Hollow logs or cavities at the base of deadfalls or under rock ledges are typical, though some bears in Yellowstone are privileged tenants of steam-heated caves among the hot springs, and a she-bear with yearling cubs may select a dry place on the open floor of a swamp sheltered by a surround of spruce trees. Black bears, however, are less concerned with being weather-proof, and some dens are no more than shallow depressions in the sphagnum moss of a dried-out marsh, lined with a few sticks and not more than four feet in diameter. A feature of many dens is their restricted size. One she-bear's retreat, lined with grass, pine-needles, leaves and bark, was no more than thirty inches in diameter; and another had crammed herself and three cubs into a cavity only three feet wide and eighteen inches high under the arching roots of a dead pine. The Swiss naturalist, Robert Hainard, has described the den of a male brown bear in a virgin forest of giant pines and great beeches at an altitude of three thousand feet in Slovenia. This was in the base of a tree that had been hollowed out by decay to form a small chamber, and was floored with pine branches still bearing green needles which the bear had torn off surrounding trees to a height of six or seven feet. But though not a very big bear, the den was so small that he appeared to be moulded into it in a squatting position with two of his feet visible beneath him.

One wonders why American black bears so very rarely den-up in hollow trees, as those in Manchuria do. That they do not is the more remarkable in view of the fact that they commonly rest and sleep in trees, especially in grizzly country, where the special trees used by them year after year as safe retreats become deeply scarred and worn. Manchurian bears make use in particular of those large poplars and limes which, though they may have broken crowns and rotten hearts, are still strong and without crevices in the lower parts of their trunks. Two or three bears have been reported occupying separate 'flats' in one of these giant poplars, which may girth twelve or fifteen feet and stand eighty or a hundred feet. The flats are from thirty to seventy feet above the ground, and before settling in, the bears clean out all the rotten wood and use this for their beds. During the winter the trees become plastered with frozen snow, so the occupant gnaws an air-hole higher up the trunk, above his flat. As temperatures fall, frost-rime collects around the air-hole, betraying the hibernating bear's presence to the hunter. If no hollow trees are available, then these Manchurian bears may, like those in America, den-up among rocks or in caves, or merely allow themselves to be snowed over on some northern slope where snow lies until March.

From time to time on the Ontario coast of Hudson Bay, a polar bear dens-up in a typical grizzly's site beneath the undercut vegetable mat at the top of a river bank or in a cavity against the upturned roots of a fallen tree in the spruce forest. But not one in a thousand polar bears dens-up in such surroundings. Their home is among the ice and the snow, and it is in October that the pregnant she-bear quits the sea-ice for the land or the land-fast ice in order to prospect for a deep snow-drift on the lee slope of a hill or valley, preferably not more than five miles from the shore – though some bears den-up in the great heaps of pressure-ice or on icebergs in fjords. In so harsh an environment the den of a polar bear must necessarily be a more enduring structure than those of forest bears, and a pregnant she-bear may wander around for a long time before she finally determines on a suitable snow-drift in which to excavate a den. As she digs down into the drift, so her place of entry is filled in with the snow she shovels behind her, and is finally sealed off by blizzards. Were it not for the air-hole that her warm breath keeps open above her sleeping place, and for the sickly-sweet odour that is emitted through it and attracts the Eskimo hunters' dogs, the den's presence in the snow-drift would not be suspected. A number of dens have been examined, and most have been found to be oval in form, seven or eight feet long, five feet wide and five feet high, with ceilings and walls firmly packed. But some dens are half as large again as this and divided into two compartments, of which one serves as the she-bear's sleeping place where the cubs are born, and the other possibly as a play and exercise room for the cubs when they are able to run around several weeks after birth. A hibernating bear engenders a remarkable heat, and the temperature within an occupied den may be as much as forty degrees higher than that without.

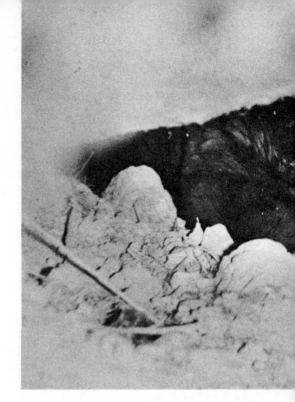

In so far as a polar bear never leaves her den for a period of from 120 to 140 days, subsisting throughout that time on her reserves of fat (and also giving milk to her cubs, warm and purring in the soft fur between her thighs), she may be said to hibernate. But neither she nor any of the forest bears pass into an advanced state of hibernation, for though their body temperatures may fall a degree or two and their heart-rate slow down a little (with the result that they become somewhat lethargic, sleeping heavily), most remain in full possession of their senses. The Canadian zoologist, C. R. Harington describes how, on a very cold February afternoon, he punched a narrow hole in the snow roof of a polar bear's den on Southampton Island in order to ascertain the temperature of its interior. When he enlarged the hole further, a glistening black eye and twitching muzzle were immediately applied to the aperture. Subsequently the she-bear paced the floor of the den, uttering peevish grunts, while her two cubs huddled against its far wall. The Eskimo hunter is well aware that it is easy to waken a hibernating bear, and having located a den with the help of his dogs, rouses the bear by plunging his seal-lance into the den. With a rumble and commotion the bear breaks out in a cloud of snow, growling angrily, and is

44

Rocky Mountains black bear in 'hibernating' den

promptly dispatched, the hunter having saved himself the labour of dragging the carcase out of the den.

American black bears are also reported to sleep lightly, alert to voices outside their dens; one that was photographed in a Rocky Mountains den in February was fully awake and moved towards the photographer. No doubt the degree of torpidity varies from one individual to another, and there is some evidence that he-bears and barren she-bears sleep more heavily than other classes of bears. One observer in California in the early years of this century describes (albeit in somewhat unsatisfactory terms) how he kept under observation a large barren grizzly she-bear throughout one winter:

I never saw her when she was not shivering like a Chinaman in an ague in the ten to thirty degrees below zero weather, and yet, to my touch, she was as warm as toast; but I could never arouse her to wakefulness, further than to make her change her position, growl, smack her chops, and blow as only a bear can, by the most severe prodding with a sharp stick. She was in a deep stupor exactly as a man 'dead drunk', and the instant that I quit prodding her, she was sound asleep.

There are widespread reports that before going into hibernation bears adopt certain measures that produce an obstruction in the rectum. A hundred years ago the Greenlanders asserted that, before denning-up, a female polar bear would contrive such an obstruction with earth, moss and grass; while the Baffin Land Eskimos believed that having first killed and cached several seals, the she-bear then ate moss, to produce this *tappen*, as they called it, before returning to her cache and gorging on blubber. Similarly, Russian brown bears are reported to form a *tappen* of their own hair, and American black bears of hair admixed with fragments of jack-pine; while according to guides and hunters, Alaskan bears first gorge themselves with 'cranberries' – thereby purging their intestines as if with soap and water! – and then eat the roots of certain plants that form a tough fibrous anal 'seal'. On emerging from hibernation in the spring a grizzly's first food is said to include the stalks of hellebore, the bulbs of the glacier lily and the excessively pungent roots of the skunk cabbage. These precipitate the evacuation of the seal. Although hellebore is poisonous and induces diarrhoea, there is no evidence that lilies or skunk cabbage are purgative. But whether or not there is any truth in this curious lore, it is a fact that black bears habitually feast on the large, sweet and juicy, purple berries of the cascara, despite the fact that these have a strong purgative effect.

Were this belief in a *tappen* not so widespread one would be justified in relegating it to the pleasant realms of folk-lore. As it is, a bear's ability (and especially that of a she-bear suckling cubs) to survive several months in hibernation without food is a phenomenon for which those natives, whose food and very existence depend upon an accurate knowledge of an animal's habits, require a simple explanation – and this belief supplies it. If there is no truth in this lore it is remarkable that approximately the same explanation crops up in localities thousands of miles apart. In this respect it is interesting to note that in both India and Ceylon sloth bears, who do not hibernate, are extremely partial to the highly laxative pods of the *Cassia fistula* shrub, the seeds of which are set in a sweet black 'gum'.

Although some polar bears with cubs may emerge from hibernation emaciated and half their normal weight, he-bears and barren she-bears of all kinds are reported, more often than not, to emerge almost as fat as when they denned-up in the autumn; and this is also true of captive black bears with cubs. Bears that break out early in the spring are no doubt those whose reserves of fat have been exhausted, and this apparent spring fat is probably no more substantial than a spongy layer of empty cells. In most cases it is lost during the first two or three weeks after emergence, when a bear must travel many miles in search of food.

It has been asserted, as we have seen, that an Alaskan bear feeds, after breaking out, on certain plants that will purge him. Whether or not this is the case, it is certainly true that most bears feed sparingly, or not at all, for a few days. Even captive black bears will do no more than put out their tongues and touch the first food offered to them, and do not eat their fill until after the lapse of three or four days or even a week. Wild black bears first nibble a little grass or cedar twigs. Polar bears, both male and female, take only grass or berries that have been preserved under the snow, before setting out in search of seals. Barren-ground grizzlies and Kamchatkan bears, who may not break out until mid-April or even May when the sun has melted large patches of snow on south-facing slopes, are content to feed for the first few days on grass and shoots in the vicinity of their dens, or merely lie in the sun without feeding. Wright, incidentally, noted the regularity with which bears of the same class would break out at approximately the same time, and cited the instance of six grizzlies in the Selkirk Mountains of British Columbia who broke through several feet of snow from six different caves on one mountainside in a single night.

This reluctance to venture far afield for food on first emerging from hibernation can be attributed to physical weakness after the long confinement in cramped quarters, and also perhaps to the need to recover from a state of semi-torpidity.

On the other hand a she-bear with cubs or yearlings must necessarily emerge in full possession of her senses if she is to protect them and obtain food for them. M. L. Peelle recounts how in the first week of April one year, shortly before the main snow-melt, he located the den of a brown bear some two thousand feet up the side of a sparsely wooded mountain on one of the Kuriles: his attention being drawn to its presence at a distance of three hundred yards by the considerable vapour rising above it. The Kuriles bears den-up in natural caves, or dig holes, early in October with the first heavy falls of snow, some six weeks earlier than those on Hokkaido (the north island of Japan), whose dens are usually in birchwoods or clumps of bamboo, with the leaves and culms of which they litter the floor to a depth of two or three feet. The only external evidence of this particular den, buried under four or five feet of snow, was a hole some eighteen inches in diameter; and when Peelle was preparing to examine it more closely, the bear's snout appeared through the snow. Almost immediately a seven-foot she-bear heaved back the snow and plunged out, to be followed by two five-foot yearling she-bears. Though lean with no surplus fat on her, she was in no way emaciated, and extremely quick in her actions, as were the cubs.

CHAPTER FIVE

Their anti-social and family life

In general all bears lead a remarkably solitary existence except in special circumstances, as when numbers of brown bears congregate where salmon are spawning, or numbers of polar bears are attracted to the carcase of a whale. But although there may be nine or ten Alaskan bears feeding in one patch of berries, or five or six catching salmon in one riffle, they cannot be said to form a social group, for they come and go singly and take no notice of one another, or pretend not to; and there is some evidence that he-bears establish private fishing territories which are not fished by other bears during the owner's absence. An American black bear behaves in the same way, making elaborate pretence (to all appearances) of not being aware of other bears feeding in the same woodland glade, looking everywhere but in their direction; and Wright gives an amusing illustration of this offhanded behaviour:

A black bear had sat down at the foot of a small pine tree and was leaning lazily against the trunk, turning its head now and then as though watching for something to turn up. It was a pretty good-sized bear – three hundred pounds or so perhaps – and when another animal of about its own size appeared some distance along the side hill and, somewhat to my surprise, began to walk threateningly toward it, I became very much interested. The first bear, however, paid, or pretended to pay, no attention whatever to the newcomer. And the latter, very deliberate but very determined, came straight toward him. When he arrived at the other side of the small tree (it was not more than six inches thick) he half drew back on his haunches, half raised his fore-quarters from the ground, lifted

Polar bear cubs are reluctant to enter the water until six months old

OPPOSITE: Polar bear society may be described as one of armed neutrality

A polar bear leads a remarkably solitary existence

one paw as if to strike, and uttered the coughing snarl ending in a rapid champing of the jaws that is the black bear's ultimate expression of wrath. But my original bear continued to lean against his tree and look about lazily as though waiting for something interesting to turn up. He did not seem to so much as suspect that there was another bear in that neck of the woods. And the challenger turned round and walked away as deliberate, as dignified, and as unconcerned as though nothing whatever had happened.

In the days when polar bears were numerous and as many as a hundred might collect at the carcase of a whale or at those of a herd of walruses slaughtered by sealers for their tusks, they too would arrive singly – witness the killing by that whaling skipper who, in one afternoon, shot thirty-five polar bears, one after the other, as they gathered at the carcase of a whale stranded on a beach in Mackenzie Bay. Polar bears, indeed, carry solitariness to such lengths that two he-bears will veer off the trail rather than face a head-on collision. Their society may be termed one of armed neutrality in which unnecessary fighting is avoided, except under the compulsion of extreme hunger. Even during the mating season in April, when bloody fights may occur, three or four he-bears trailing a she-bear, by picking up the scent of her frequent urinatings, usually do so at a considerable distance one from another. Mated pairs of most bears keep company for only a month or less, though sloth bears (and perhaps spectacled bears) are an exception, since males and females of this species are frequently seen together except when the latter have cubs. Since it is obviously difficult to keep track of individual bears in the field over a long period, the duration of the mating may well have been underestimated, and according to Holzworth this may, in Alaska, extend to at least two months.

Although large bears, such as Alaskan bears and polar bears, are not fully grown until they are six or eight years old, all she-bears are sexually mature at the age of three. Forest bears mate during the spring or summer in all parts of the world except apparently the Himalayas, where black bears are reported to mate in the late autumn. During the month or so of the mating season the deep barks and long drawn-out melodious calls of sloth bears, like hounds baying, are constantly to be heard from males fighting; and roaring grizzlies are to be seen in groups of four or five and occasionally fighting. They fight with their teeth, slashing and raking with those formidable fangs, while clinching each other round the neck with their immense paws, one blow from which, landing between the eyes, is sufficient to kill a bull. Although mated pairs of both black bears and grizzlies appear very affectionate, hugging, pawing and wrestling with each other, and grazing nose to nose, their affection is short-lived; and a grizzly she-bear may mate with two he-bears if an intruder is powerful enough to supplant her first mate. Since she-bears and he-bears come together only for this brief period during the mating season, one assumes that for the remainder of the year they maintain more or less separate feeding territories, except when gathering to the berry harvest, to spawning salmon or to carrion.

It has long been known that both brown and black bears follow the same trails through forest and tall grass, through dense thickets of willows and alders in watercourses, and along the salmon streams (well back from the river, so that they can walk in cover), day after day, year after year, for fifty years or more, until these are deeply worn. Trails first blazed by man and then abandoned may subsequently be kept open by bears for decades. Unlike deer, who follow the easiest route,

American black bears make elaborate pretences of bluffing

The black bear's ultimate expression of wrath

bears forge straight ahead without deviation through the most rugged country and up grades as steep as one in two; and in Kamchatka their trails are, or were, the only roads for travellers from one isolated village to the next. Where an Alaskan bear's trail mounts over banks or deadfalls, steps are fashioned by every passing bear placing his huge feet (fourteen inches long by ten in breadth) in the prints of those who have passed before, until the circular tracks may be ten or twelve inches deep and the trail finally pounded into parallel ruts.

It has also long been known that both brown and black bears are in the habit of 'blazing' prominent trees along these trails. This they do by rearing up and biting or clawing the bark as high up the trunk as they can reach, which in the case of an Alaskan bear will be upwards of twelve feet from the ground. Marking-trees are often those with light-coloured bark such as aspens, and individual trees are known to have been employed for this purpose for ten or twenty years. A black bear may be seen examining the lower part of a trunk for several minutes with much attention, while looking around from time to time and sniffing the air. Then rising on his hind-legs and approaching the trunk, he embraces it with his fore-legs and scratches the bark with his teeth and claws for several minutes without a break, while his jaws clash against each other until a mass of foam runs down both sides of his mouth.

Since bears are predominantly solitary animals, and undoubtedly maintain personal territories in greater or lesser degree, they might reasonably be expected to employ some method of indicating the boundaries, though since every bear's pad-prints are as individual as a man's finger-prints, these presumably constitute one form of recognition. For a hundred years or so, right up to the present year, most naturalists have believed that bears mark trees for this purpose, as wolves and cats urinate against posts and trees. Some confirmation of this belief is suggested by an incident recounted to Dufresne by two Alaskan hunters, in which a he-bear, having come out on the trail ahead of them, glanced back at them without apparent recognition and continued on his way until he came to a small hemlock. There he stopped to rub his back against a limb, and then reared up to his full height and tore loose a large strip of bark. Then he swung boldly round to stare at the men, before dropping down and disappearing among the trees. His 'warning' mark could hardly be reached with the extended muzzle of a rifle. John M. Holzworth, who lived with Hasselborg on Admiralty Island while photographing bears, has recounted a similar incident.

Some naturalists, both ancient and modern, have gone so far as to suggest that since the largest bears (and also tigers and jaguars) can reach highest up a tree, the height of their marks will be appropriately significant to smaller bears that pass that way. Perhaps this opinion is based on the words of an old hunter: 'Only he-bears bite trees. They bite them along the roads, and the one that makes the tallest marks, bosses the road. After you kill the big one, you don't see another he-bear for a long time on that road. She-bears pass any time.'

This statement recalls the tale of one of Wright's contemporaries of a clever but dishonest young bear who rolled a stump up to a marking-tree and, by standing on this, was able to put his mark so far above those of his fellows that he terrorised all the other bears in the forest.

No doubt tree marking is predominantly a masculine habit. Nevertheless, it is a habit shared by she-bears; and these trees also serve moulting bears as scratching posts for their backs when they are ridding themselves of their winter fur in early summer – at which season they are also to be seen rolling on gravel beaches with all four legs in the air. One is bound to say that the observations of other old North American hunters do not support the view that blazing trees serves any territorial purpose – or does not always do so. Wright, who witnessed the act on three occasions, laughed to scorn both this hypothesis and particularly that of warning by height. Consider in this respect his account of tree marking by grizzlies, who employ teeth only. He describes how on an August evening he saw a she-bear and two yearling cubs come out of a canyon and begin feasting on berries. They were followed by a large he-bear, and subsequently by a smaller one, who appeared to be only half awake. On reaching the edge of the timber, the latter looked indifferently around, sat down and scratched his ear with his hind-foot:

He then got up lazily, sniffed up and down the trunk of a small fir tree, stretched his paws upward, and, raising himself on his hind feet to his extreme height, set his teeth into the small trunk and yanked off a chunk similar to those I had seen scattered along the

Food is a problem for grizzlies in the spring

OPPOSITE: Grizzly chasing a beaver

Barren-ground grizzly scratching a moulting back

trail. This was all done in the most unconcerned and bored manner imaginable, without any show of ugliness or temper. There was nothing to indicate in the least that the brute intended the act as a defiance or a challenge to any other bear. He acted as if he had nothing to do and was hard pressed to pass away the time. Afterwards he walked out to where the other bears were, and joined them at berry-picking. The other male bear paid no attention whatever to the action.

On another occasion I saw two three-year-old grizzlies peacefully ambling along a hillside. They would walk along for a short distance, stop and sniff at stumps, scratch a little, and then move on again. After a time they came to some trees, and one of them stood up with his paws against a trunk, smelled quite around it, turned his head sideways, drove his teeth through an inch or more of wood, and with a twist of his head ripped off a slab. He then sniffed at the open place, lapped it a little with his tongue, dropped down on all-fours, and followed the other bear.

If a bear does not mark trees as a territorial indication, what other reasons might he have for doing so? It could be merely a physical expression of wellbeing in the stretching and relaxing of muscles as a cat does, releasing tension, delighting in strength. (There is more than one record of an Alaskan bear biting a tree with such fury as to fracture a bone in his lower jaw.) If one accepts Wright's estimate of the black bear's character, it could be merely an expression of boredom. It could also be for the purpose of manicuring and blunting claws, grown long and brittle during hibernation. Seton described, for instance, an encounter between two Adirondacks guides and a very large black bear newly emerged from hibernation. Following the bear's back trail through the snow for a couple of hundred yards from the stream where he had taken his first drink, they came upon a small pine tree that had been deeply scored by the teeth of a bear at a height of five or six feet from the ground. Indeed, so many slivers had been freshly torn out of the tree that the bole had almost been bitten through. A hundred yards further on the trail ended at a great hollow pine tree, which proved to be the bear's winter den.

Consider also Wright's observation about the three-year-old grizzly that sniffed at the wound he had made in the tree and then lapped it with his tongue. Now, black bears, after emerging from hibernation in the northern Rockies, are in the habit of tearing large hunks of bark out of lodge-pole pines; while in Washington State they peel the sweet and sticky cambium bark from second-growth Douglas firs. One lodge-pole pine in every ten may be ringed in this way by bears, and according to Cahalane the inner bark of various species of pines has tonic properties. On the other side of the Atlantic, Bulgarian brown bears also habitually strip the bark from pine trees after emerging from hibernation, ringing them to a considerable height; and the peasants agree with Cahalane in believing that they do so in order to benefit from the tonic effect of the rising sap.

The normal litter for most she-bears consists of two cubs, though as many as four or even five or six are possible, and young bears usually have only one cub. Whether it be in a den on an iceberg or in a hollow log in a Malayan jungle, the cubs are usually born between December and February, though sometimes not until March, after a prolonged gestation due to a delay in the implantation of the ovary in the uterus. At birth they are, as we have seen, minute in relation to the size of the she-bear, being only from seven to twelve inches in length and one or two pounds in weight. European brown bear and American black bear cubs leave the den two months after birth, but those of Manchurian black bears and polar bears will not do so for three or three and a half months, during which period they have, of course, been fed exclusively on their mothers' milk. Unseasonable snowfalls may delay the break-out. As late as 21 June one year Wright encountered deep snow-drifts in the Bitter Roots mountains of Idaho and watched a black bear and her three whimpering five-pound cubs ploughing through the soft slushy snow. The cubs, however, were continually falling into the large holes made by their mother's feet, and from time to time she would have to sit down and wait for them.

Very few men have seen a she-bear breaking out of her den in the spring. But Dufresne has described how a hunter in Alaska in May saw through his binoculars 'a snow-drift come pushing up, split into petals like those of an unfolding daisy, and out of the center into the bright sunlight came the yellow head of a Peninsular grizzly'.

After breaking out, this she-bear then reached back into the hole and lifted out a cub which, however, scuttled back into the hole when she reached in for a second cub. Both cubs kept

Some European brown bears have a habit of 'ringing' trees

scuttling back into the hole in this manner, until the she-bear finally plodded some distance away from the den and slumped down comfortably against a bank of snow. It was not long before the cubs emerged and made their way over to her to be suckled. After she had fed them, the she-bear led them slowly away from the den, along a snow cornice overhanging several hundred feet of sheer space. One cub scampered to the edge, but recoiled in fright and ran back to hide under its mother's belly. But the other cub, after crawling to the edge, stretched out its neck to peer over. Soon it was joined by the other cub, and side by side they hung head down, gazing at the vast new world below:

Further down from the pinnacles the she-bear took her ease on an exposed flat rock while the cubs wrestled and played tag. A steep snow-filled chute was the perfect place for sitting on their rumps and sliding like a couple of boys on bobsleds. Over and over they climbed back to do it again until one of the descending youngsters scooted full tilt into the other. Squalling with rage, they tore into one another tooth and claw, and mother had to lambaste them with her heavy paws to start them once more on the long journey to the green strip of meadow at tidewater.

By the time a polar bear breaks out of her den in March or April her cubs, now two or three feet in length and twenty or thirty pounds in weight, can run almost as fast as a man; but for the first few days the family make only short excursions away from the den, returning to sleep in it at night. During this period the cubs strengthen themselves by play, with the entrance passage to the den serving as a practice climbing pitch and the nearest ice-slope as a toboggan run. Sliding down on their bellies, legs spread-eagled, they are caught again and again in the paws of the she-bear stationed at the bottom of the run. No doubt this preliminary interval for strength through play is a feature of bear life in general. American black bear cubs, when they emerge and cannot yet walk steadily, play incessantly; and despite their uncertain gait can climb like cats to the top of the tallest tree.

The pleasurable habit of play continues into adult life. One polar bear will rock himself on a drifting ice-floe. Another will climb to the top of a large tilted floe and lie down on his side, before giving a push with one paw and sliding down thirty or forty feet, to strike the water with a great splash. After climbing out he walks sedately away. A third will sit back on his

European brown bear cubs leave the den two months after birth

haunches at the top of a steep bank of hard snow against the
face of a cliff, and steadying himself with his forepaws,
glissade to the bottom.

Young bears in particular are always likely to perform some
crazy action. Dufresne saw a young grizzly high up at the head
of a snow-packed ravine 'doing a balancing act along a wall
of ice. Suddenly, it jumped off onto the almost perpendicular
slope and came zooming out on the slick, wet ice of the glacier
at a dizzy rate of speed. Then, to my complete amazement, it
came sailing over the lip of the glacier to plunge fifty feet into
a lake. Apparently none the worse, the young grizzly paddled
ashore and started climbing the slope again.'

So too, on a day some fifty years or more ago, the naturalist
Enos Mills watched a grizzly tobogganing down a steep
mountainside in the Rocky Mountain National Park:

As he sat down in the snow, put his fore-paws on his knees, and
jiggled himself along to start, he appeared strangely human. At one
point he reached back his paw and put on brakes. He ended the
'coast' with a jump and somersault. Then, selecting a different place
on the slope, he started down again, pushing himself along with
both fore-paws to get up speed. He ended this time by deliberately
rolling over and over. Rising on hind feet, he looked at his marks
on the snowy slope and climbed back up for another coast.

One might not perhaps suspect that the surly and sometimes
savage adult bear could relax in play or that he would be
innocently interested in the activities of other animals; but
when the pressure of man, the killer-in-chief, is off, and food is

Two cubs are the normal litter

American black bears are constantly on the look-out for grizzlies

OPPOSITE: A grizzly on elk kill

plentiful, then play and idle moments are no doubt indulged in more frequently than is generally supposed. In the spring or in the late autumn, an Alaskan bear will sit for hours on a high crag, from which he can survey the surrounding country, while swinging his massive head from side to side slowly and with dignity. Another will sit back on his haunches, dog-like, and watch with interest a family of otters tobogganing down a mud slide or beavers working at their dam. American black bears have been reported playing with coyotes, even of attempting to play with the irascible porcupine – often unwisely – and Mills describes an encounter between a grizzly, forty miles from his home range, and a skunk. Waiving his right of way, the grizzly went into a siding some fifty feet from the trail, and sat down to wait for the skunk to arrive and pass. Bored with waiting, he began to clown, throwing a somersault and rolling in the grass, before sitting up like a young puppy to watch the skunk pass.

When the polar bear family finally leaves the den and sets out for the sea-ice to hunt seals, the cubs show remarkable powers of endurance in keeping up with their mother. Generally they follow stoutly behind her in single file, but in deep snow (since they stand only from nine to sixteen inches at the shoulder), they keep beside her in order not to fall into her enormous tracks. But she does not allow them to become too tired, pushing them up hillocks with her muzzle between their hind-legs or sometimes carrying them on her back. (A sloth bear normally carries her cubs on her back, to and from the feeding grounds, as soon as they are strong enough to grip her fur; and if alarmed when feeding they scramble up on to her back again and bury their faces in her fur. Some sloth bears carry their cubs until they are as large as spaniels, though in these cases there is usually only room for one cub on the mother's back, and the unlucky one must follow on foot.)

During the first few days of the polar bear family's journey to the sea-ice, the she-bear stops frequently to play with the cubs, ducking them in the leads of open water, sliding with them down the sides of small icebergs, tumbling and scrapping in the snow with them, or suckling them on the sunny side of a block of ice or large rock. From time to time she climbs a hummock from which to survey the surrounding country, and if she spots any suspicious object, leads the cubs off the trail

A sloth bear carries her cubs on her back to and from the feeding grounds

A female polar bear with cubs is wary of encounters with other bears

on a circuitous detour. She is wary of encounters with other polar bears, for there is some evidence that he-bears will kill, though not eat, cubs; if danger threatens she spanks them along before her. Polar bears cover such immense territories that the chances of a he-bear and she-bear with cubs meeting are not very great. Among the Alaskan brown bears, however, cubs are not infrequently killed by he-bears, and there may surprisingly be some cannibalism of she-bears and smaller bears during the mating season. One suspects that this occurs only under abnormal conditions – when, for example, the victim is in a trap. A report in *Animals* describes the experience of two Kodiak guides in May 1958. Their attention was attracted by a she-bear (with a cub) who was peering over the edge of a bluff into a ravine. The reason for this behaviour was explained when a large he-bear came into sight, following her trail slowly up the ravine. On seeing him approach, the she-bear began to climb up a snow slide, pausing from time to time to wait for the cub; but the soft snow and the very steep slope soon tired the cub, and it finally halted after running for some thirty minutes. The he-bear climbed slowly up to the cub and, grasping it by the head, shook it from side to side. When the cub was dead he began to shred the carcase and devour it. Then, after burying the remainder of the carcase in the snow, he began chasing the she-bear, who had in the meantime been sitting only two hundred yards away, and followed her over the high crest of the snow-covered ridge.

Clearly this kind of behaviour must be the exception rather than the rule, or bears would long since have ceased to exist. Nevertheless, cases of cannibalism have also been reported among the brown bears of Kamchatka, and there is also a record of a large American black he-bear breaking into the den of a smaller bear, killing and eating it, and taking up temporary quarters in its den.

According to the old American hunters, all she-bears are in the habit of spanking their cubs, and one describes how, when he was crossing a mountain stream with a pack-train of mules and was sighted by a grizzly she-bear, she 'clattered' to her cubs to come down from their tree. As soon as they came down, she spanked them over a distance of two hundred yards until out of sight. In contrast to the apparent lack of communication between a black bear and her cubs, a grizzly grunts continually to hers when on the trail.

Dufresne watched an Alaskan brown bear with three cubs negotiating a glacial torrent in the Valley of Ten Thousand Smokes. While the cubs fretted anxiously, the she-bear picked each one up in turn by the scruff of its neck and carried it across. But when, a few minutes later, they balked at a mere rill, she spanked them soundly on their rumps and sent them bawling through the shallows.

An American black bear will dispatch her cubs up the nearest tree whenever she wishes to be rid of them and wander away to feed on her own. When danger threatens, especially in wolf or grizzly country, she will cuff them severely if they disobey her, and they will stay up the tree for hours, playing and sleeping, until she calls them down again. If they are directly threatened, she endeavours to lure the enemy into following her away from the tree. Polar bear cubs are normally so obedient, abandoning their play and 'freezing' in an instant into immobility, that one wonders in what way she communicates with them. But spanking may be considered a necessary means to survival, impressing on the cubs the correct way to stalk a seal if they are budding polar bears, to dig out a

Male American black bears have been known to kill cubs despite females' defence

The spectacled bear's survival is probably not endangered in the forseeable future

OPPOSITE: Two families of polar bears

ground squirrel if they are grizzlies, or to avoid such dangerous animals as men or bull walruses or pumas.

But she-bears can also be affectionate. Dufresne stresses this, to him unexpected, tenderness in referring to one of the rarest sights he ever saw in the wilderness on a summer's day, above the tree-line of Admiralty Island. He describes how he was sitting on a rock ledge a hundred feet or so above a well-travelled bear trail when twin brown bear cubs suddenly bounded into view. Behind them swaggered the she-bear, unaware of human presence and at peace with the world. On reaching a grassy hummock almost directly beneath him she sprawled herself on it and gave a low call. The cubs immediately came leaping back and, snuffling into the hair of her breast, found themselves a nipple each and began suckling lustily. While they suckled she groomed each of them from head to foot with her tongue, before leaning back and apparently falling asleep. After the cubs had nursed their fill, the family meandered out on to a sloping hillside and settled down to feed among the lush over-ripe blueberries.

Providentially for polar bear families it is in March that the ringed seals give birth to their pups in chambers below the ice and under three or four feet of snow, and though there is virtually no external evidence of these birth chambers, the

American black bear and cubs watching male

she-bear's wonderful nose enables her to locate them with almost unfailing regularity. Having found one she proceeds to excavate most of the overlying dome of snow very rapidly with quick blows of her paws. Then, rearing up, she plunges down on the *aglo* with the whole weight of her body on her forelegs. She may have to pound the *aglo* again and again before being successful in breaking through its hard-frozen dome. Then she thrusts in her broad paw and hooks the pup out with her claws.

The families stay out on the sea-ice throughout the summer and autumn, though some she-bears with cubs who have been born on islands can be marooned on them if the land-fast ice breaks up early in the spring, for the cubs are most reluctant to enter the water until they are six months old. While the she-bear stalks seals, they sleep or play. Not all cubs, however, are amenable to discipline and 'stay put'. Peter Freuchen, that superhuman Arctic explorer, observed that the stalk of a sealing bear might be seriously hampered by her cubs' disobedience, for if the stalk was protracted the cubs might become impatient and begin moving about. At this, the she-bear would return and cuff them violently, before beginning her stalk all over again. But just when she was about to make her final rush they might begin to move again and frighten the seal into escaping into the water.

All young bears remain with their mothers for considerable periods, and polar bears may suckle theirs for as long as eighteen months. Yearlings, during their second winter, usually den-up with their mothers, or in their own dens a few yards distant from hers. There are intervals of two or three years between litters, and it is no doubt the he-bear, when the she-bear comes into season again, who ultimately breaks up the family. An Alaskan hunter described to Dufresne how early in June one year he saw a grizzly come over the top of a hill and make a deadline for a she-bear accompanied by two two hundred pound yearlings. On sighting him the yearlings squalled in fear; but their mother ignored them, allowing the he-bear to sniff at her, while she nipped his neck. Then, as she moved away, he fell in behind her, nudging her persistently and occasionally rushing open-mouthed at the cubs. It was not long before the latter went their own way.

An American black bear will despatch her cubs up a tree whenever she wishes to be rid of them

CHAPTER SIX

Their enemies

Bears are less affected than most large mammals by the activities or hostility of other animals in their territories, and with individual exceptions they have no enemies except man, though smaller bears may be in some danger from larger bears inhabiting the same range. Black bears are, for example, killed by grizzlies, and are constantly on the lookout for them, seeking refuge in trees immediately they wind or hear them, and long before the human observer is aware that grizzlies are anywhere in the vicinity. When both inhabit the same country, black bears do much of their feeding by day, since grizzlies tend to come abroad towards evening. Nevertheless, as many as a dozen black bears may play jackal to a grizzly in possession of the carcase of a sheep or a cow.

At some time in the distant past, however, bears must have been preyed upon by some dog-like carnivore, for all bears are inherently afraid of dogs, and a couple of terriers will put a grizzly to flight. It is significant that when a grizzly is travelling he still has the habit of circling back off the trail at intervals, in order to get to windward of his own back tracks. He may indeed make a detour of as much as a mile, and then stand quietly for some time, taking stock. But few bears have any present cause to fear dogs or wolves, though no doubt that scourge of Asian jungles, the hunting pack of wild dogs, occasionally tear sloth bears and sun bears to pieces, as they do tigers. Russian brown bears are occasionally attacked by wolves (and are also driven from carrion by that ferocious killer whom the largest carnivores fear, the wolverine.) One

OPPOSITE: A Himalayan black bear can defeat a tiger in a fair fight

of the large polar wolves may kill a polar bear cub when its mother is away hunting, and a small pack of them may harry a he-bear into abandoning his seal kill. But there are no records of adult polar bears or grizzlies being killed by wolves, though a hunter described to Dufresne a unique encounter between wolves and grizzlies he witnessed in the Mt. McKinley National Park, when he was watching a den where a small grey she-wolf had her cubs. The wolves had buried a number of game carcases near the den, and the smell of these attracted a she-bear and her three three hundred pound yearlings. One of the latter sniffed to within thirty feet of the den, outside which the she-wolf and the three cubs of the previous year's litter were crouched, and seizing the carcase of a caribou, began dragging it down the hill. At this, all four wolves set upon the young bear, and subsequently upon the she-bear when she came roaring to the defence of her cub. The bears eventually fought their way clear to a nearby knoll, and that might have been the end of the affair, had not another of the yearlings smelled out a second buried carcase. In the meantime the large black male wolf had returned from hunting; and he, after touching noses briefly with his mate, launched himself against the she-bear, while the other wolves renewed their attacks on the young bears, particularly on the smallest, who was weakening. On becoming aware of the plight of the latter, the she-bear broke away from the male wolf and, roaring hideously and laying about her with swinging paws and snapping fangs, drove the three cubs down into a patch of thick brush and through it into a glacial stream. There the small one, lame and dripping blood, lay down up to its neck, while the other three backed into the water until the wolves were out of their depth and broke off the engagement.

In America a few black bears are killed by pumas. Although averaging not much more than one hundred and fifty pounds in weight, a puma is such an agile carnivore that it can compete on equal terms with the much more massive jaguar; but one would not expect it to threaten a grizzly weighing up to nine times its own weight, and accounts by the old mountain hunters of the American West indicate that most pumas, though bristling and growling, would edge off the trail and give the disinterested grizzly the right of way. Similarly, when feeding on its kill, a puma, though snarling and spitting in the most threatening manner and holding its place until a grizzly

OPPOSITE: Polar bears are perpetually wandering from one country's international waters into another's

The restless hibernating black bear

was within a few feet, would ultimately surrender the kill. It would strike at the bear as it dashed off, but the latter would not even bother to take notice of its going.

Nevertheless, an occasional grizzly is shot with long, deep scars on its back; and the fact that a medium-sized one may sometimes be killed by a puma is indicated by the account of an army officer hunting with two Apaches on the Pecos during the last century. According to Seton, they had tracked a large puma to a canyon, where their attention was attracted by a fearful din:

A middle-sized brown bear was standing on his hind-legs with his back against a big rock and was yelling bloody murder. The lion was crouched on the ground about twelve or fifteen feet from the bear. They waited there quite a while, the lion in the position of a cat about to spring, working his tail, with his ears laid back and getting ready for a jump as he moved his feet back and forward, as you will see a tomcat do. Once in a while he would growl. At last the lion charged the bear and grabbed him, and they both went down together and the dust flew up so that it almost hid the two fighters. In a little while the lion suddenly let go and sprang back to where he had been before. Both animals were bleeding and each was licking its wounds. The bear kept up his moaning and screaming and would have been mighty glad to get away, but he did not dare to expose his back to the lion. At last the lion charged the bear again, and this time with his claws he tore open the bear's back, and his claws must have reached some deadly part, for presently the bear fell over dead and the lion went off to his old place and began to lick his wounds again. After a while he took hold of the bear's carcass, and began to drag it down the hill and cover it up with leaves and brush.

The only predator which may possibly have taken a significant toll of bears at one time is the tiger. The Russian, N. A. Baikov, describes how the large Manchurian tigers which in his day, in the early years of this century, grew to a length of twelve or possibly thirteen feet and to a weight of six or seven hundred pounds, could handle brown bears of almost their own weight, by stalking and ambushing them on a cliff or in a fallen wind-break. When an unsuspecting bear ambled into the ambush, the tiger would spring on it from above, seize it by one paw under the chin, by the other at the neck, and would bite through the vertebrae. Should a bear sense danger in time, it would take refuge in the nearest tree. In this case the tiger might wait under the tree for the bear to grow impatient and descend, but would more often feign a departure and hide-up nearby until the bear came down, when it would attack again.

Since Baikov had thirty years' experience of hunting and exploring in Manchuria we must accept his statement that a tiger will mimic the mating call of a female black bear in order to lure the he-bear to him. But more remarkable is the statement of another Russian, Krements, that a bear will also employ these tactics, in support of which he gives an astonishing account of a bear 'calling up' an elk (wapiti) during the rutting season:

On 27 August I was hunting a large elk in a remote spot at sunset. It immediately responded to the call of the forester standing fifty to sixty paces behind me, and after rubbing its horns on the trees in a perfectly audible fashion the elk moved forward with a constant bugling. I stole up under cover towards the animal. When only sixty to seventy paces away, I unexpectedly heard a strange sound from the dense thickets slightly reminiscent of the call of an elk. It sounded dubious even to me, because of its high pitch and lesser purity of tone. Repeated several times, the call forced the elk to cease its own bugling, throwing it into a state of confusion. At the same time, the creature which produced the sound moved quite rapidly toward the elk; this was clearly heard from the sound of breaking twigs. It charged forward noisily, roaring powerfully. The elk turned rapidly and fled. Approaching very close, I saw clearly a bear of medium size catapulting over a small forest clearing towards the fleeing elk some twenty-five yards from me.

In India numbers of sloth bears are killed by tigers, though a sloth bear is not an adversary to be taken lightly, for given the opportunity it can inflict fearful injuries with its long claws, blunt though they are. But when the tiger is the predator the opportunity does not occur, for the tiger stalks the bear from the rear while it is feeding, and seizing it by the nape of the neck forces it to the ground. The average sloth bear, being more exclusively vegetarian than most bears, does not expect to attack or be attacked, or to have relations with any other animal. This may be inferred from his behaviour in the jungle where he is extremely noisy, crashing through the undergrowth, bubbling, squealing, squeaking and grunting, as he turns over stones in the moonlight.

In the Himalayas, a case occurs from time to time of a tiger preying on bears, both black and brown. Nevertheless, some of the very large black bears of that region are powerful enough to achieve the incredible and defeat a tiger in fair fight. Jim Corbett watched a tiger and an exceptionally large black bear fighting over the former's kill. His account of this unique experience throws a most unexpected light on the bear as a predator. The tiger had been eating for a quarter of an hour when Corbett caught sight of the bear strolling along the crest of the hill:

Suddenly he stopped, turned facing downhill, and lay flat. After a minute or two he raised his head, sniffed the wind, and again lay flat. The wind was blowing uphill and the bear caught the scent of flesh and blood, mingled with the scent of the tiger. Presently he got to his feet and, with bent legs and body held close to the ground, started to stalk the tiger.

He had possibly two hundred yards to go and though he was not built for stalking, he covered the distance as smoothly as a snake and as silently as a shadow. The nearer he got the more cautious he became. I could see the lip of the fifteen-foot drop into the hole, and when the bear got to within a few feet of this spot he drew himself along with belly to ground. Waiting until the tiger was eating with much gusto the bear very slowly projected his head over the lip of the hole and looked down, and then as slowly drew his head back. His opportunity came when the tiger was cracking a bone. The bear drew himself to the edge and, gathering his feet under him, launched himself into the hole with a mighty scream – to be answered by an even mightier roar from the tiger. The fight may have lasted three minutes, or it may have lasted longer. Anyway, the tiger broke off the engagement and came along the open ground in front of me at a fast gallop, closely followed by the still screaming bear. Blood from a number of deep cuts was seeping through the thick fur on his neck and in several places his scalp was torn right down to the bone, his nose being torn in half.

A superficial acquaintance with the colossal polar bear would lead one to suppose that this was a bear who had nothing to fear from any inhabitant of his world of ice and snow. So far as land predators are concerned this is true enough. He is the master of his environment, moving with astonishing agility through deep snow and much faster than any other animal at speeds of up to 20 or 25 mph over the roughest sea-ice, with the dense hair on the soles of his paws and their short strong claws gripping the slightest fracture in the glass-like surface of the wind-polished ice; leaping nimbly, despite his immense bulk, over six-foot high ice hummocks and scaling with apparent ease the steepest and roughest pressure-ridges of the pack. He treads warily, however, over new sea-ice, scrambling across patches of this on his belly with legs spread-eagled. But ironically, despite a polar bear's virtuosity in the water where, with broad paws serving as paddles, he can cover one hundred and eighty yards a minute, cavorting like a porpoise in ten or twelve feet leaps, he is so helpless in this medium that even a troop of young ringed seals will gang up on him, nipping at his flanks and forcing him to make for the nearest ice-floe at his best speed.

During the summer, polar bears kill numbers of young walruses, either when the latter are lying out on the rocks, or by swimming submerged and seizing them when they pop their heads out of the water to breathe or look around. But a bull walrus, fifteen feet in length and a ton or a ton and a half in weight, is a very different proposition. Rarely indeed will a bear attack a bull, even when the latter is lying out on the ice and comparatively helpless. For that matter, a bear attempting to kill a young walrus may be set upon by a dozen cows and gouged to death by their twelve-inch tusks. The superiority of the bull walrus over the polar bear has been known for centuries – not that walruses prey on bears in any sense of the word, though an occasional cub may be killed by a bull on the ice. But should the two chance to meet in the water, then the walrus is invariably the killer, striking downwards with his thirty-six inch tusks into the bear's back or flanks, and dragging him under water when, as hunters graphically put it, nothing of the bear comes up again except small scraps of skin with white hair.

It will be recalled that polar bears are usually reluctant to swim over stretches of open water. Indeed, except when hunting seals, they normally take to the water only in emergencies – when attacked by sealers or harried by aircraft; and it may well be that this reluctance is due to their fear of walruses and also of killer-whales. The latter, with their fearful battery of from twenty to twenty-eight teeth capable of shearing a porpoise in half or tearing the side out of a white whale, are even more formidable enemies than walruses, being intelligent enough to heave a floe deliberately up and down with their backs in attempts to pitch a bear and her cub (or a man for that matter) into the sea.

Polar bears are reluctant to swim over stretches of open water

CHAPTER SEVEN

Relations with man

Despite being constantly hunted, Russian bears often take up quarters near villages and even den-up near them or near footpaths frequented by villagers: just as on Wrangel Island, in the east Siberian sea, polar bears den-up only a few hundred yards from the settlement, and can be watched from the school house windows playing with their cubs when they break out from their dens in March.

Bears, in the main, are neither carnivorous nor aggressive towards man; and although there have been many stock-killing bears, there has never been an ursine parallel to the man-eating cat. Nevertheless, many men have been killed by bears, and in exceptional cases partly eaten by polar bears. Even the small sun bear has the reputation among animal collectors of charging on sight, and is more feared by them than the tiger, who normally prefers to give man the right of way. But this reputation is based in fact on the reactions of a very few and no doubt previously wounded individuals, for most sun bears are timid, and even she-bears with cubs endeavour to escape rather than attack in their defence.

Stock killing by the individual carnivore can prove to be the first step on the primrose path to man killing, and instances of Himalayan villagers being mauled or killed in sudden encounters with stock-killing black bears are reported every year. The next step is, when losing his caution of man, a bear takes to raiding stock-yards in broad daylight, and comes into direct conflict with him. Such behaviour is particularly associated with the late autumn when natural food sources are

OPPOSITE: The temper of a polar bear is unpredictable

becoming scarce, but when some bears may not have fattened up sufficiently to go into hibernation. Those barren-ground grizzlies, their fur heavy with ice, whom the Indians and Eskimos encountered during the winter, were especially feared. On Hokkaido, a bear that has not denned-up by December is recognized as dangerous, since in his quest for food he will kill all kinds of domestic stock, even rabbits and chickens, and also attack humans, especially in sudden encounters at dusk or on foggy days when crossing the trails of horsemen or lying-up in the bamboo grass near paths. So too, the Kamchatkan villager does not go out after dark without shouting a warning of his coming when non-hibernating bears are known to be about. Bears who break out early in the spring because their reserves of fat are exhausted may also, being ravenous, be dangerous.

Of course a she-bear *may* charge you if she thinks that you constitute a danger to her cubs. Even the relatively 'friendly' American black bear will not always consider harmless the photographer who sets up his tripod within twenty-five yards of her when she is feeding with her cubs. One out of three grizzlies with cubs is euphemistically described as exhibiting 'strong protective instincts'. Sloth bears are savage and quick in defence of their cubs, and in one unprecedented instance a

One out of three grizzlies with cubs exhibits strong protective instincts

she-bear with two almost fully grown cubs not only became a man-killer for a period of six weeks, but apparently ate portions of her victims. No doubt there was a special reason for this uncharacteristic behaviour, but precise details of the incident are lacking. More characteristically, rather than defend their cubs by direct attack, both black and brown bears attempt to escape immediately or to frighten away the intruder by growling and leaping at him. Heaven knows, with ears laid back and hair bristling along nape and back, their mien is impressive enough. They may actually abandon their cubs if the latter are too young to run with them. Even when wounded, they will not necessarily attack, though if, after wounding a cub, the hunter has sought safety in a tree, the she-bear may shake the tree vigorously in an attempt to bring him down.

Of course a he-bear may attack you, if you blunder on him when he is feeding, or when he is sleeping in a thicket after a meal of salmon. Before entering cover where bears are known to rest, the wise man announces his coming – when any bear he disturbs will either make off, or work off his anger in a blood-curdling moaning that goes deeper and deeper as the minutes pass. But in ninety-nine cases out of a hundred, whether he be an Alaskan giant or a sloth bear, he attacks, or simulates an attack, either because you have impeded his getaway, or from fear, or because he is confused. This is especially likely to be the case in dense cover where neither party has a clear view of the other, particularly since some species of forest bear are short-sighted, or do not distinguish objects with precision at close range.

Possibly some bears do not hear very well either, if a sloth bear's noisy progression through the jungle be any criterion. Despite his very small external ears a sun bear's hearing is also acute and he is responsive to sounds barely audible to man.

Grizzlies, too, have excellent hearing. Indeed, their widespread habit of smashing beached canoes is popularly believed to be due to their curiosity being aroused by hearing the reverberations of their own footfalls in the shells of canoes covered by snow, which incites them to dig down to the canoes and right through them! They also have good sight, though since their small eyes are set far forward, their lateral field of vision is restricted. But the final arbiter of judgement

Rearing up on hind legs, he regards man attentively

is the nose, with which a grizzly can detect the scent of a man fourteen hours after the latter has crossed a trail. On hearing or seeing a strange object, a grizzly usually rises on his hind legs in order to obtain a better view: but he rarely determines on his course of action until he has also tested the nature of the object with his nose by circling down-wind. All bears have to be given time in which to weigh up and work out a situation, and Holzworth describes how Hasselborg was in the habit of reprimanding an angry bear loudly until the latter turned away grumbling into the forest. If a man's scent is a sloth bear's first warning of his presence, then he flees instantly. If he is up a tree he will, on sighting a man, slip round to the other side of the trunk, drop to the ground – in a fifteen-foot fall if necessary – and make off at a gallop, keeping the trunk between him and the hunter. But if an unfortunate woodcutter stumbles upon this ordinarily inoffensive bear without warning, then the bear attacks in blind fear, swiping with his claws and also using his teeth. It is because of the ever-present possibility of such accidental encounters that the villagers in Ceylon fear the sloth bear as the most dangerous animal in the jungle, and those old men who have survived such attacks with faces almost torn away are living witnesses to the truth of this. Bears, one should perhaps note, do not kill their victims by hugging, but by biting or sometimes by striking with round-arm swings of inward-curving paws. Nor do they normally rear up in order to strike as generally depicted but, whether grizzly or sloth bear, go for a man on all-fours, as they do when fighting each other.

Naturally, a bear alarmed or angered by a sudden encounter, is still more likely to attack if the intruder runs away – though who would not run from the horrific apparition of an angry bear with small red eyes glowing balefully and rubbery black lips bared back from yellow fangs! And the immense size and horrific aspect of one of the great brown bears, towering ten or twelve feet when erect, is no doubt responsible for the legendary killer reputation of the grizzly. If provoked he is indeed a terrible foe, and Eskimo hunters speak with much greater respect of the relatively small barren-grounds grizzly, which seldom reaches a weight of eight hundred pounds, than they do of the polar bear. For half a million years the large brown bears have dominated the forest life of North America, and have long been accustomed to raid the

Indians' tepees for cached food. It is only during the past two hundred years that a new kind of man, able to kill at long range with high-powered rifles, has challenged their domination.

Considering the grizzly's reputation, it is a most remarkable fact that the early nineteenth century hunters were unanimous in stating not only that he never attacked a man except when surprised or provoked, or when suffering from an old wound, but that he invariably fled at the sight or scent of a man. Even when suddenly encountered, he would rear up on his hind legs threateningly and, breathing heavily, would regard the man attentively for some time – providing that the latter stood his ground – and then turn away and gallop off. Similarly, when a grizzly scents the carcase of a buck in a hunter's camp, and comes stalking in with horrendous roars, he no doubt expects the hunter to abandon his buck without a fight – as a smaller bear might reasonably be expected to do. Even if he presumes further, and pokes his colossal head through the tent wall, he will still not attack, if the hunter has the strength of will to lie motionless. Coming, as it does, from hard-bitten old-time hunters, this is indeed unexpected tribute to the true nature of the grizzly. 'From all my experience the conviction is pressed upon my mind that the grizzly-bear possesses a nature which, if taken in time and carefully improved, may be made the perfection of animal goodness', wrote John Capen Adams. In the 1850s Adams travelled and hunted the South-west with four or five tame grizzlies whom he had reared from cubhood, and one of them, Ben Franklin, fought in his defence when he was attacked by a very much larger wild grizzly. Those trappers and hunters, however, whose cabins and gear have been wrecked by the appallingly destructive strength of a grizzly, attracted by the stench from dumps of carcases or decaying food, would not share this opinion!

The grizzly of the old-timers was of course the smaller bear of the plains and eastern Rockies, not the giant of Alaska. Contemporary estimates of the grizzly's character vary, depending no doubt on the individual's personal experience, or lack of experience, and also on the particular region in which he was working or hunting. On the one hand are those who agree with the old-timers that he is cautious, even timid, and prefers to run rather than attack; and that if he does charge, he will not necessarily do so to kill. David Bardack, for

A grizzly has to be given time in which to weigh up a situation

There is always the bold individual: silver-tip grizzly

instance, describes in *Animals* an incident in which he was the 'victim' in the summer of 1966, when he was engaged in field-work on the barren-grounds of the Northwest Territories. On his attention being attracted by a yearling caribou walking slowly across his path, only thirty feet ahead of him, and stopping every few steps to look behind it, he noticed that it was being followed by a she-bear with two cubs. When the bear caught sight of him she turned and walked towards him. Being unarmed, Bardack ran down the hill to a shallow stream some twenty-five feet below. There, he looked back up the hill in the hope that as he had left the immediate vicinity of the cubs, the she-bear might have lost interest in him. But she came over the crest and ran down the hill towards him. Shouting to one of his companions, with a view to distracting the bear, he then splashed into the stream. The bear, however, followed him across, came up to his side and, still on all-fours, grasped his right elbow lightly in her jaws. The shock of this and the muddy footing caused him to slip to the ground, but instead of mauling him, the bear halted for only a second or two before running around him and then back across the stream and up the hill to her cubs. His injuries amounted to no more than slight cuts and scratches where the bear had taken hold of his elbow.

On the other hand, according to Dufresne the giant brown bears of Alaska, and particularly the more carnivorous bears of the Kenhai Peninsula, are often aggressive and have made more unprovoked attacks on man than any other bears – though one has always to keep in mind the possibility, or probability, that aggressive bears may have previously been shot at and wounded. But Dufresne's experiences in Alaska are contrary to those of Cahalane – who found that all the bears he encountered fled on sight, with the exception of one who continued on his way, indifferent to Cahalane's presence – and also to those of Hasselborg and Holzworth. Holzworth photographed some seventy-five bears at a range of less than fifty yards, and a further twenty-five at less than twenty yards, but was only twice charged – indecisively. Hasselborg, who killed more than two hundred bears over a period of thirty years, was only charged a dozen times – by wounded beasts.

Their experiences with Alaskan bears were very similar to those of Andy Russell, the Alberta game-guide and photographer, with barren-ground grizzlies, for he and his sons photographed bears in the Yukon for two years without ever carrying a gun, and at one period had two hundred meetings with bears in three months. Although they filmed many of them within a range of a hundred yards and some within fifty yards, they never considered themselves to be in real danger, though sometimes they had to take avoiding action.

The truth of the matter probably is that while most bears are wary when confronted with an unknown animal such as man, there is always the bold individual who is the exception.

In recent years there have been several cases of hikers and campers in the National Parks being severely mauled, and even killed in their sleeping-bags – an event that no nineteenth century grizzly hunter would have credited. There cannot be any doubt that this abnormal behaviour is instigated by tourist pressures in National Parks, by a general ignorance of animal habits and psychology, and by man becoming too familiar an object. 'If one had to live ten years in bear country', declared one American old-timer, 'there would be much more danger of being struck by lightning than of being injured by a black bear.' Yet black bears in National Parks have now become so familiar with tourists and with the tasty foods they bring that they are inveterate cadgers, not only acting and clowning in order to obtain these, but sometimes, if refused, taking them by force and breaking into cars and cabins in order to purloin tins of food, sugar, flour, beans, or bacon.

In dealing with bears one has always to remember that all have uncertain tempers, and that therefore their behaviour is never predictable; and none more unpredictable than polar bears. One will run away from a pack of husky puppies; another will do the same immediately it gets the wind of a sledging party a quarter of a mile distant. But a third will charge a man without provocation – the only indication that he is about to do so being a slight wrinkling up of his nose. Since he is a true predator, one would expect his behaviour towards man to differ somewhat from that of other bears. But this is not the case. As with the grizzly, one is impressed by the polar bear's reluctance to kill when a man is at his mercy. There are several records of one overtaking a man running away, only to lope off without striking him; while if a man stands steady, a charging bear may lose interest before actually reaching him, or, having reached him, may still do no more than sniff at him. If, over the years, many Eskimos have been

killed by polar bears, the great majority of them have been hunters killed while lancing or knifing bears at close-quarters. Other Eskimos have been killed because, when squatting motionless beside an *aglo*, they were mistaken for seals. In *Wild Animals of North America*, E. W. Nelson tells the story of two Eskimos who had gone out to attend to their seal nets, which were set through holes in the ice:

While at work near each other, one of the men heard a bear approaching, and having no other weapon but a small knife, the bear being between him and the shore, he threw himself upon his back upon the ice and waited. The bear came up in a few moments, and smelled about the man from head to foot, and finally pressed his cold nose against the man's lips and nose, and sniffed several times; each time the terrified Eskimo held his breath until, as he afterwards said, his lungs nearly burst. The bear suddenly heard the other man at work, and listening for a moment, he started towards him at a gallop, while the man he left sprang to his feet, and ran for his life for the village, and reached it safely. At midday, when the sun had risen a little, a large party went out to the spot, and found the bear finishing his feast upon the other hunter, and soon dispatched him.

Most attacks of this nature take place during the winter when bears are hungry or starving. But normally a polar bear's sole interest in man is the potential edibility of his possessions, whether these be dogs, sledges, caches, boats or dwellings, and not in man himself. Every explorer has emphasized the polar bear's intense curiosity in them and their belongings, and his habit of following sledging parties for miles at a discreet distance; and Eskimo hunters take advantage of this curiosity, shouting and waving in order to attract his attention. A bear will even scale the deck of a ship, frozen-in for the winter, in order to pilfer the meat hung in the rigging; and, if not met with the customary hail of bullets, he will take food proferred to him on a boat-hook or thrown over the side. Man's activities in the Arctic – the settlements of Eskimos and Chukchees, the food caches of explorers, and especially the offal of sealing parties and whaling stations – must periodically have significantly influenced the distribution of polar bears. But, as the Russian zoologist S. M. Uspensky says, 'self-defence can no longer be tolerated as an excuse for killing a polar bear who can be effectively scared off by rockets or flares.'

OPPOSITE: Every explorer has emphasized the polar bear's intense curiosity

CHAPTER EIGHT

What future for bears?

In those still immense, inaccessible areas of forest in Asia one presumes that bears still go about their business as they have done for millennia, and at least some Abominable Snowmen may in reality be brown bears – or red bears as they are known throughout the Himalayas – for many of the tracks of these snowmen lead to the burrows of pikas which, as we have seen, are extensively preyed upon by the blue bears of the Tibetan and Mongolian steppes.

Beyond the wilderness, the plight of bears is, in general, that of most other large mammals. In India sloth bears were, like tigers, quite extraordinarily numerous a hundred years ago; but from the middle of the nineteenth century they were slaughtered by officers of the Indian Army and Indian Civil Service with revolting callousness. It was not as if they afforded 'sport'. They were used for target practice or shot when there was nothing better to shoot by trigger-happy sahibs. Although not at present included in the International Union for the Conservation of Nature's red list of animals in danger of extinction, sloth bears no longer inhabit many Indian jungles where they were once common, and yearly retreat deeper into the remaining jungles. In Ceylon their habitat is endangered by the widespread felling of forests to make room for massive resettlement schemes for an expanding population; and while they have been protected in the National Parks since 1964, their chances of survival outside the Parks must be considered doubtful.

The wholesale felling of forests in Malaya, and the popula-

OPPOSITE: A European brown bear has survived forty-seven years of captivity

Polar bears have lived for forty years in captivity

tion explosion in Indonesia, must also be threatening the survival of the sun bear – which apparently also inhabited Ceylon until about a hundred years ago. Sun bears damage only one of man's possessions – his coconut plantations – and there is little demand for their skins. They are persecuted almost solely for the price they realise in the vast Chinese quack-medicine trade – a curse responsible for the decimation of wildlife throughout Asia, and beyond.

Disafforestation in the Andes has also begun to cut back the habitat of the spectacled bear. However, much of the latter's range is so inaccessible that its survival is probably not endangered in the foreseeable future. It is a commentary on how little we know about many of the larger mammals, that it is still necessary to refer to the notes on the spectacled bear made by the explorer Jacob von Tschudi during his travels in

Peru more than one hundred and twenty-five years ago.

It is a thousand years since the last brown bears were killed in Britain, though they are perhaps still remembered in the word *beiste* (beast) which occurs in place-names here and there in the Scottish Highlands, in what must once have been typical bear country. That a very few thousand brown bears still survive in the natural forests of the remoter mountainous zones of Europe can be ascribed to their adaptability, omnivorousness and preparedness to travel long distances in search of food. Longevity may also be in their favour, since a brown bear has survived forty-seven years in captivity, and Wright kept track of a wild grizzly for more than twenty years. (Both sloth bears and polar bears have lived for forty years in captivity.) But against these survival advantages must be weighed the disadvantages. Theoretically, a she-bear might produce a dozen cubs in a lifetime, and a captive brown bear has in fact given birth to a cub in her thirty-first year. In the wild state, however, few bears are likely to reach this optimum, and the long interval between litters constitutes a threat to the survival of any small population of mammals. Further disadvantages are that every hunter in Europe wants to kill a bear above all other beasts of the chase, and that some bears give others a bad name by becoming embroiled with shepherds and villagers over livestock losses. It has also been suggested that the widely scattered nature of Europe's small communities of bears may result in some she-bears not being found by he-bears during the mating season, with the result that her interval between litters is still further extended. This possibility does not seem very likely, however, having regard to a bear's willingness to migrate long distances, and to what must be a he-bear's strong urge to mate with she-bears that come into season only once in three years.

Whether wild bears can continue to survive in over-populated Europe is anyone's guess; or for that matter in the Near East, where a few of those biblical raiders of vineyards from the Caucasus to Palestine still inhabit Syria, Iraq and Iran. We do not need to search far for the causes leading to the virtual extinction of this particular race of brown bears, for it was (and to our shame, still is) the race that produced the unhappy performing bear – and also targets for the soldiers of two world wars. (There is reasonable evidence that another race of brown bears inhabited the Atlas Mountains in North

The unhappy performing Syrian brown bear

European brown bear cub

Africa until some fifty years ago; but there has been no factual news of these for more than a century, and no specimen has ever reached a museum. Also, according to native sources, there was once a bear, the 'kaurai', in Abyssinia.)

The hard fact is that Europe's surviving communities are dangerously small. Between sixty and eighty bears are reported to remain in the Pyrenees; no more than a score or so in the Italian Dolomites, where forests are being felled on a large scale and the habitat further destroyed by the construction of dams and facilities for tourists; and between forty and sixty in the Abruzzi National Park in the Apennines.

In Finland their numbers have been reduced to no more than one hundred and thirty, after the slaughter of six hundred during the past ten years. Under an iniquitous law, any Lapp marking the den of a hibernating bear acquired the exclusive rights to that bear, and was prepared for a fee of up to £1000(!) to guide a foreign sportsman to the den, and then drive the bear out so that it could be shot. Whether a new protection law, operating between mid-October and mid-April, will exercise any significant check on this slaughter remains to be seen.

In Sweden bears enjoyed complete protection until 1943, when an annual open season for hunting of two months was introduced. By 1957 their population had been reduced to an estimated two hundred and twenty residents, augmented by a score or two of wandering bears. This level, however, has been maintained during subsequent years and, now that the inhabitants of northern Sweden and Lapland are being encouraged to emigrate from their isolated settlements to larger communities in the south, it is possible to anticipate an increase. As the settlements are abandoned, so cultivated areas revert to forest; at the same time, it is becoming uneconomic to fell the forests in the far north and transport the timber south. Lowland coniferous forests in the south and east are being recolonized, and bears are becoming common near some settlements in the south of Lapland, while the two main habitats in Sweden, which have been isolated for the past hundred years or so, have now amalgamated.

During the past twenty years there has been an increase in the number of Swedish bears wandering into the southern and central northern regions of Norway. Even so, the total population of bears in Norway is estimated to number only from twenty-five to fifty, of which ten or twenty in the Vass-faret forests north-west of Oslo comprise the sole permanent breeding population. Since these forests are being felled and new roads are being driven into the area, it must be considered doubtful whether this community can survive, particularly as there is still, throughout Norway, only partial protection of bears.

In south-east Europe since 1934, and after protection had been granted to all except habitual stock-killers, there has been a fifty per cent increase in the numbers of Bulgarian bears to a population of some four hundred and fifty. Extensive felling of the natural forests in the mountains must again, however, drastically reduce the area of their habitat and force them to emigrate. They may go southwards to Greece, or westwards into Yugoslavia, where bears are protected and increasing in the great forests of oak, beech and spruce in Dalmatia. Alternatively, they may go northwards into the Rumanian Carpathians, where the bear population is estimated to have trebled since before the war to a total of some three thousand five hundred. It was in the Carpathians in the autumn of 1955 that what must be the most remarkable gathering of bears anywhere in Europe during recent years was recorded. In the course of a beat of some six hundred and seventy-five acres of mountainside at a height of some two thousand feet, ninety-eight bears were counted on the wooded slopes and valleys.

Who would care to predict how much longer brown bears and grizzlies will survive in North America? Formerly their range stretched from Mexico's northern plateau, through the Rockies, the Sierra Nevada and the Cascade mountains, to Alaska and its islands and the Arctic shores of the Northwest Territories. Early in the nineteenth century it was said that thirty or forty grizzlies might be seen in a day: but within seventy-five years of their first contact with the covered-wagon pioneers they had been virtually wiped out. In 1922 the last of the large 'golden' grizzlies was killed in California. Today, despite partial or complete protection, grizzlies are extinct to the south of the USA-Canadian border, except in the National Parks and in a few isolated areas such as the Chihuahua mountains of Mexico where, however, the small grizzly of that region has been almost exterminated by hunters with hounds.

Today, the USA population of grizzlies (excluding Alaska,

where there may still be ten thousand) numbers less than six hundred, one-third of whom are in the Yellowstone National Park. So too, in the Northwest Territories the barren-ground grizzlies are particularly vulnerable to hunters in spotter aircraft; and during the years 1960–64 the suspension of all protection resulted in such a severe culling that their population had been reduced to about five hundred by 1966. How near this population figure is to being non-viable may be realised when one considers that, of this total, only one hundred may be breeding she-bears yielding an annual increment of at most seventy cubs, against which must be set a total loss by natural mortality and human kill of sixty-five.

In view of this real possibility of the barren-grounds grizzly becoming extinct, the Canadian Wildlife Service initiated in 1965 (when too late?) a study of all the factors upon which their survival depended. Two years earlier, American zoologists had experimented with marking grizzlies in Yellowstone, by trapping them in portable steel culverts, baited with honey, bacon and pineapple juice. They were successful in capturing and drugging two bears, to whom they affixed miniature transistors attached to plastic collars. The transistors' bleep had a range of five miles, and it was found possible to follow one grizzly night and day for a month despite snow-storms. The CWS, however, are employing foot-snares, which slow up a bear sufficiently to allow a member of the research team to administer a drug by means of a syringe fired from a crossbow. The bear is then ear-tagged with numbered red, yellow or green streamers.

In America, as in Europe, the brown bears have been driven into those areas more or less inaccessible to man, of which the Mackenzie mountains in the Northwest Territories are an extreme example. Lying partly within the Arctic Circle, snow-covered for eight or nine months of the year, and with temperatures as low as −70°F, conditions are too severe for much human activity or ranching. But even in these natural sanctuaries the bears are persecuted. In Alaska, for example, the protracted open season from 1 September to 20 June brings in hunters by plane and motor-launch to shoot bears grazing on the 'meadows' before they can escape into the forests of the hinterland; and there has been an immense reduction in their numbers during the course of this century.

It is possible that nowadays *controlled* hunting may present

Last refuge? Barren-ground grizzly and cub in
Mt MacKinley Park

a less serious threat to the brown bears' survival (and also to
that of other bears) than the widespread activities of cattle
ranchers, commercial fish canners, and especially the US
Forest Service's logging contractors, which are ruthlessly
destroying their habitat on a vast scale.

Alone among those whose habitats have been encroached
upon by man, American black bears have been sufficiently
resilient and adaptable to withstand his persecution. True,
their population has probably decreased by sixty per cent
during the past hundred years; but in the USA, despite no
protection outside the national parks and despite the activities
of some twenty million hunters and pop-gunners, they still
inhabit all but four States of the Union, and one estimate puts
their number at upwards of two hundred thousand, with
perhaps as many again in Canada. Their continuance in such

numbers must be due to a fundamental survival factor that is not immediately apparent, though they may perhaps have benefited by the extermination of their chief enemy, the grizzly.

In view of the black bears' success it appears all the more remarkable at first sight that polar bears, so far removed from man *en masse*, should have suffered the same fate as grizzlies and European brown bears. Polar bears were formerly as essential to the Eskimos' economy as brown bears were to the Kamchatkans, and in a few remote Arctic regions they still are. Their hides made waterproof pants, boot-bottoms, sleeping robes and sled-covers, and with fragments of them the Eskimos polished their sled runners. Their flesh fed the huskies and sometimes men. But the toll taken by the few Eskimo peoples scattered around Arctic shores in no way affected their numbers, and the journals of the seventeenth century Dutch and English mariners indicate that they were remarkably numerous. Nevertheless, it was in the seventeenth century, when whalers first penetrated the Norwegian and Russian sectors of the Arctic, that their survival as a species began to be threatened. Then, as whaling declined, the sealers with their better-equipped boats killed still larger numbers. Trappers were an even greater menace, for they supplied the Eskimos with rifles and encouraged them to trade furs.

Since the 1920s there has been a catastrophic decrease in the world population of polar bears, the limits of their range have contracted, and throughout the Arctic more than a thousand are still being killed annually – many by commercial and safari hunters using spotter aircraft to kill bears on the ice off Alaska. In addition there is a large trade in live cubs in the Norwegian Arctic, and *cubs can only be taken alive after the she-bear has been killed*. Today, there are a thousand polar bears or more in the world's zoos, representing probably about one-tenth of their world population. But a major difficulty in enforcing laws passed for their protection and conservation is presented by the fact that being such inveterate nomads, they are perpetually wandering from one country's territorial waters into another's, making the problem of their conservation an international rather than a national one. During the past eight years Norway, Russia and Canada have had teams in the field researching into the possibilities of conserving the existing stock of polar bears. One can only hope that this awakening of conscience has not come too late.